Over 100 Ideas for Outdoor Numeracy

Key Stages 1 & 2 Teacher Resource
By Maylie Dickerson

Published by Thinking Child
Website: www.thinkingchild.org.uk

Information and enquiries: 01604 491511
info@thinkingchild.org.uk

Cover Illustration by Kris Lillyman, Imagine Studios

Printed in the UK by Print Projects Northampton Ltd.

978-0-9575388-3-2

Introduction

Welcome to this book which is packed with exciting ideas to help you deliver maths outdoors.

Learning outdoors can be hugely beneficial especially when used as part of a whole school or curriculum approach.

It creates opportunities for

- larger physical movements – space to move around more freely which is known to have a positive effect on children's learning.
- the promotion of the 'feel good factor' from being in the fresh air – this is not to be underestimated
- emphasising the playful elements of learning – having fun whilst learning can be very memorable.

All the ideas in this pack are written to make maths relevant and purposeful with many direct links to real-life situations. They have been found to be particularly useful for children who sometimes struggle with classroom based maths, offering a fresh dimension through this active engagement with learning.

The activities are intended for teachers to incorporate into medium and short term planning cycles and will no doubt be added to over time.

They are not just a means to just take 'indoor learning outdoors' but to enhance ways of delivering the maths curriculum as a whole. Any large space is suitable for many of these sessions, if weather is ever a real issue.

The pack caters for KS1 and KS2 and is linked directly to the primary maths curriculum but, as the developmental stages of real children don't always neatly match these, it might be necessary to use professional judgement: to change, adapt and experiment with the ideas to fit your own context.

They could work very well as activities for small targeted groups working with a TA or other classroom helper – with minimum training.

The grid at the beginning of the pack provides an overview of the activities and they are alphabetically ordered and cross referenced to the specific areas of the curriculum, giving a quick overview of content and coverage.

In this way you will be able to achieve a balance over time and more easily slot them into your planning as a whole.

There is sufficient material here to allow every year group an outdoor maths session every week of the year.

The activities have been designed to need minimum preparation and to use equipment that is readily available in most schools.

However, some do require resources that need to be made but these can be used many times over and become a bank of shared school resources.

We really hope that the ideas in this book prove to be a useful and enjoyable for all your staff and children.

Have Fun!

****

Things to remember:

Risk assessments – should be done every time you use your outdoor spaces – just a quick check with your site agent or caretaker to make sure things haven't changed in any way since you were last out there.

Do you need to negotiate the boundaries with children for each session?

The aim is for children to independently use their judgement, according to the activities, but you may also need to judge whether children need a verbal boundary or sometimes a physical boundary such as rope or a chalk line, whilst on that 'journey to independence'.

Activity	Number Place Value	Addition Subtraction	Multiplication Division	Fractions Decimals Percentage	Geometry Shape	Geometry Position Direction	Statistics	Measure	Ratio Proportion	Algebra	Problem Solving	Cross curricular links
3D Skeletons - *3D shape properties, measuring length activity*					3 4 5 6			3 4 5 6			✓	*DT Science*
10 Green Bottles - *measuring volume, capacity, problem solving activity*	1 2							1 2			✓	
All the Shapes in the Bag - *shape recognition and properties, direction game*					1 2	1 2						*PE*
Beat the Ball - *reciting numbers, sequences and multiples games*	1 2 3 4 5 6	1 2 3 4 5 6	1 2 3 4 5 6									*PE – gross motor skill*
Beds and Borders – *measuring length, perimeter, area, problem solving activity*					5 6			5 6			✓	*Geography History DT*
Bird Cakes – *standard and non-standard measures activity*								1 2				*Science*
Car Park Conundrums – *measuring length, perimeter, area, volume, problem solving activity*								2 3 4 5 6			✓	
Car Park Data Collection - *data collection, measuring length, problem solving activity*							2 3 4 6				✓	
Castles in the Sand - *estimating mass, problem solving activity*							6	1 2 3 4 5 6			✓	*Seaside*

Activity	Number Place Value	Addition Subtraction	Multiplication Division	Fractions Decimals Percentage	Geometry Shape	Geometry Position Direction	Statistics	Measure	Ratio Proportion	Algebra	Problem Solving	Cross curricular links
Days and Months – *language relating to days of the week and months of the year*								1				*Literacy*
Divide and Conquer - *division and factors in multiplication game*			1 2 3 4 5 6								√	
Double the Fun - *doubling - multiplication by 2 activity*			1 2									
Everything in Order - *Ordering numbers and objects activity*	1 2 3 4											
Fee Fi Foe Fum - *measuring length and time, problem solving activity*		1 2	1 2					1 2			√	*PE Literacy*
Find the Fractions - *fractions, decimals and improper fractions games*				1 2 3 4 5 6								
Find Your Way Home - *fractions, decimals, percentages, measuring length and volume game*						1 2 3 4 5 6					√	*Seaside Space*
Frivolous Fractions – *equivalent fractions, decimals, percentages, measuring length, volume game*				5 6				5 6			√	

Activity	Number	Addition Subtraction	Multiplication Division	Fractions Decimals Percentage	Geometry Shape	Geometry Position Direction	Statistics	Measure	Ratio Proportion	Algebra	Problem Solving	Cross-curricular links
Fuelled Up - *measuring capacity, multiplication and division activity*			5 6					5 6			✓	
Funfair - *money, addition, subtraction, problem solving games*		1 2 3 4 5 6						1 2 3 4 5 6			✓	*PE – eye/hand coordination*
Get Together – *number facts to 10,20,100, multiplication, problem solving game*		1 2 3 4 5 6	2 3 4 5 6								✓	
Go the Extra Mile – *measuring length, conversion, problem solving activity*								5 6			✓	
Gridlock – *coordinates game*						4						*Geography*
Guess the Weight of the... *estimating and measuring, converting mass game*								4 5 6				
Hang it Out – *number sequences game*	1 2 3 4 5 6	1 2 3 4 5 6	2 3 4 5 6	5 6								
Hide and Seek – *number facts to 10, to 20 game*	1 2 3 4	1 2 3 4									✓	
Hot or Cold – *measuring temperature. Collecting and recording data, line graphs activity*	1 2						1 2 3 4 5 6	1 2 4 5 6				

Activity	Number	Addition Subtraction	Multiplication Division	Fractions Decimals Percentage	Geometry Shape	Geometry Position Direction	Statistics	Measure	Ratio Proportion	Algebra	Problem Solving	Cross-curricular links
I Spy Shapes – *shape recognition game*					1 2 3 4 5 6							*ICT*
Ladders – *number facts, doubles, halves, odd and even, multiples game*	1 2 3		2 3 4 5 6									
Let's go Fly a Kite – *shape and angles, measuring length, recording data, problem solving activity*					3 4 5 6		3 4 5 6	3 4 5 6			✓	*Science DT*
Let's Grow – *measuring length, perimeter, area, problem solving activity*								1 2 3 4 5 6	5 6		✓	*Science*
Logistics – *measuring volume, capacity, algebra, problem solving activity*								5 6		5 6	✓	*Transport*
Make a Bolt for it – *measuring length, ratio, recording data, line graphs activity*							5 6	5 6	6			*PE PHSE Science*
Make a Mint – *money, place value, problem solving game*	1 2 3 4 5 6							1 2 3 4 5 6			✓	
Mass – *estimating, measuring mass, greater than, less than activity*								1 2 3 4				

Activity	Number	Addition Subtraction	Multiplication Division	Fractions Decimals Percentage	Geometry Shape	Geometry Position Direction	Statistics	Measure	Ratio Proportion	Algebra	Problem Solving	Cross-curricular links
Match Box Competition – *four operations, ordinal numbers, fractions, percentages, collecting and recording data, problem solving activity*	1 2 3 4 5 6	1 2 3 4 5 6	4 5 6	4 5 6			3 4 5 6		6		✓	
Multiple Choices – *multiplication, division, fractions, percentages, problem solving activity*			1 2 3 4 5 6	2 3 4 5 6							✓	
Nature Search – *addition game*		1 2									✓	
Operation Inverse – *addition, subtraction, multiplication and division. Inverse operation game*	1 2 3 4 5 6	1 2 3 4 5 6	3 4 5 6								✓	
Pairs – *number facts to 10 game*	1 2 3 4	1 2 3 4									✓	
Paper Boy – *odds and evens activity*	1 2										✓	
Photo Shoot – *multiplication, problem solving activity*			3 4								✓	
Pi – *shape, algebra, problem solving activity*					6					6	✓	
Play Dough – *measuring mass, volume, non-standard measures activity*	1 2							1 2				*DT Art*

Activity	Number	Addition Subtraction	Multiplication Division	Fractions Decimals Percentage	Geometry Shape	Geometry Position Direction	Statistics	Measure	Ratio Proportion	Algebra	Problem Solving	Cross-curricular links
Playing Card PE – *Counting. Mental addition, multiplication and division activity*	1 2	1 2	3 4									*PE*
Pop! – *measuring capacity, volume, problem solving activity and game*								3 4 5 6			✓	
Pot and Pans – *measuring capacity, multiplication, problem solving activity*			4					4			✓	
Shape Hunt – *shape properties game*					1 2 3 4 5 6							
Slalom Run – *multiplication and division game*			2 3 4 5 6									
Sort it Out – *Carroll diagrams activity*							3 4					
Spell Check – *read and write number in words activity*	1 2 3 4				1 2 3 4 5 6							
Sports Weigh In – *measuring mass problem solving activity and game*								5 6			✓	*PE PSHE*
Squash – *problem solving, measuring length, perimeter, area, shape activity*					1 2 3 4 5 6			1 2 3 4 5 6			✓	

Activity	Number	Addition Subtraction	Multiplication Division	Fractions Decimals Percentage	Geometry Shape	Geometry Position Direction	Statistics	Measure	Ratio Proportion	Algebra	Problem Solving	Cross-curricular links
Targets – *mental addition and subtraction game*		1 2 3 4 5 6		4 5 6								*PE*
Time and Duration – *telling time and time durations practical demonstration*								1 2 3 4				
Turning Point – *shape and angles activity*					3 4 5 6							
Twins – *number doubles and halving game*	1 2 3 4	1 2 3 4										
Venn Diagrams – *Venn diagrams, multiplication division activity and a game for Year 6*			3 4 5 6				2 3 4 5 6					
We're All Going on a...Bus Trip – *money, time, giving change activity*		3 4 5 6						3 4 5 6			✓	*Geography Literacy*
What the Time Mr Wolf? – *telling the time game*								1 2 3 4 5 6			✓	
Wheels on the Bus – *money, counting, addition, giving change activity*	1 2	2						1 2			✓	*Any subject*
Selection of Ideas for Outdoor Maths												

10 Green Bottles

Numeracy Focus: *Measurement – capacity. Problem Solving*

Suitable for: KS1 in pairs

What you will need: *Year 1* – Water tray; 10 empty plastic bottles of different sizes - with lids and labels removed but the capacity written on in permanent marker. Some examples found in most homes:

38ml (food dye); 100ml(shampoo); 200/250ml (fruit drink); 330ml (drink); 500ml; 750ml (squash); 1000ml; 1500ml; 2000ml; 3000ml (large squash); green food dye and water.

Year 2 – Water tray; 10 empty plastic bottles of different sizes as above but no capacities written on; green food dye and water; laminated cards with the different capacities written on to match the bottles; measuring jugs with clear markings.

What you do:

Year 1 – Children fill up all the bottles with green water and tighten the lids. Ask them to place them in order - from the largest to the smallest.

Talk about the numbers on the bottles. What do they notice?

Ask them to pick one large and one small bottle – how many small bottles will fit in the big bottles?

Ask them to test their predictions and say what happens.

Year 2 - Children fill up the bottles and measure the water in measuring jugs. They then match the bottle with the laminated card and put all the bottles in order of size.

Talk about the different ways we can say how much is in the bottle and ask them to repeat the vocabulary i.e. 1000ml or 1litre. Talk about abbreviations.

To extend it for more able children, ask how they think we would write 2000ml and 3000ml in litres? What about 1500ml?

Give them some unmarked bottles and ask them to estimate and then use their own methods to find out how much is in each.

They can show their results by writing their own number cards and making a display where they match their labels to the bottles. Make sure they use the ml and l abbreviations.

Back in the classroom you could give them three pictures of bottles and show them how to use the symbols > and < to order them.

Learning Benefits:

- Active, messy learning
- Real – life objects
- Prediction and Investigation
- Supports NC 2014 Programmes of Study for Maths

****

3D Skeletons

Numeracy Focus: *Geometry - 3D shape properties. Measurement – length. Problem Solving*

Suitable for: KS2

What you will need:

A large play space; lots of newsprint, newspapers or large sheets of paper; masking tape masking (one that can be easily torn); 3D shapes or real-life examples of 3D shapes; tape measures or metre sticks marked with centimetres.

What you do:

Ask children to make large 3D models of the shapes you provide them with. The task emphasises knowledge of the number of edges and vertices.

First, show them how to roll paper so that they have strong 'straws' to build with.

Take a piece of paper and start to roll it very tightly diagonally from the corner.

A good method is to fold over the corner a little way and fold the fold again and again until you have a hard cylinder to roll. Use both hands like you would roll play dough into a sausage.

When you have rolled the whole sheet tape the corner down.

Make sure the roll is really tight – it will be no good for building if it is loose.

It takes some practice but it is a good test of patience and persistence and is good fine motor skill practice.

Year 3/4 - cylinder / pyramid / cube / cuboid / cone / triangular prism

Possible Starter Questions:

Can you predict how many rolls it will take to make a cuboid?

How many for a pyramid?

Will you have to cut them to length or join two together?

Year 5/6 - other polyhedrons – hexagonal prism / octagonal prism / tetrahedron / dodecahedron?!

Starter Questions:

How many rolls do you think might be needed for a hexagonal prism?

Can you make a cylinder or a cone?

How might you join up the edges? (use the flat paper)

Who is brave enough to have a go at a dodecahedron?

Further Challenges:

Who can make the tallest structure out of the paper rolls?

Which shapes are strongest for building?

Learning Benefits:

- Active learning
- Builds fine motor skills
- Encourages skills of prediction, hypothesising, collaboration and persistence /determination
- Supports NC 2014 Programmes of Study for Maths
- Cross-curricular links - Science

****

All the Shapes in the Bag

Numeracy Focus: *Geometry - shape recognition and direction*

Suitable for: KS1

What you will need: A large play space; a bag of large 2D or 3D shapes

What you do:

This can be whole class or split into two groups.

The children make a big circle and you allocate shape names to each of them, in order around the ring.

For example; circle square rectangle hexagon pentagon – repeat the pattern until you get to the start again.

The children have to remember what shape they are.

The adult pulls a shape from the bag and all those shapes run clockwise around the circle until the adult shouts 'Home' and they continue running around the circle and back to their place.

The last one back is 'caught' and has to go into the middle.

When you have about 6 in the middle the caught shapes can be freed and re-join the game if they can each name a shape that you pull from the bag.

Continue to call the names of the shapes but occasionally shout 'anti-clockwise' before you shout 'Home' and they all have to turn round and run in that direction.

Occasionally show one shape and then another in quick succession so that you have more children racing.

You could shout properties of shapes instead of holding up an actual shape.

For example;

Year 1 – simple properties

Year 2 - 'four equal sides' for the squares or 'two sets of parallel sides' for the squares and the rectangles to run together.

<u>Learning Benefits:</u>

- Active learning
- Health benefits
- Supports NC 2014 Programmes of Study for Maths
- Cross-curricular links - PE

****

Beat the Ball

Numeracy Focus: *Number - reciting, patterns and multiples*

Suitable for: KS1 and KS2 – Whole class divided into groups of 6 to 8 of similar ability.

What you will need: Large play space and balls or beanbags.

What you do:

Children make a circle and then say which activity/maths concept you want them to do.

The children throw the ball / beanbag around the circle with each child saying the correct number when they throw the ball.

If a child gets their turn wrong then the rest of the team can help by shouting out the right number and play continues. That child still runs round the circle and back to their place before the ball / beanbag gets to them again.

- *Year 1/2* - reciting numbers to ten / twenty / fifty / one hundred / odds / evens forwards and backwards.
- *Year 1/2* - multiples of 2 / 5 / 10 and 3 and 4 (higher ability) - both forwards and backwards.
- *Year 3* - multiples of 2 / 3 / 4 / 5 / 8 / 50 / 100 forwards and backwards.
- *Year 4* - multiples of 6 / 7 / 9 / 25 / 100 / 1000 / count backwards through zero to negative numbers / Counting from any number in 2's / 3's / 4's.
- *Year 5* - all of the above / counting forwards and backwards in powers of 10 to 1,000,000.
- *Year 6* - all of the above.

Taking it further / Problem Solving /Thinking:

- Give children a starting number and an operation for a sequence i.e. x2 +1. (differentiate according to ability)
- Give children higher starting numbers for counting on such as 127 for Year 3 and 4000 for Year 5 (depending on ability)

Learning Benefits:

- Active when reciting.
- All have to think whether the answers are correct and therefore are less likely to 'zone out'.
- They are active participants even when it is someone else's turn.
- Supports NC 2014 Programmes of Study for Maths.

****

Beds and Borders

Numeracy Focus: *Measure - length, area and perimeter. Problem Solving.*

Suitable for: Year 5/6 — This links with other activities in the book: **'Squash'** **and 'Pi '**

What you will need: Information tags from flowering plants — real or make them with info from the internet; real plants that will act as examples of size, if you have them already in and around the school; coloured cards; heavy florist wire or similar.

What you do:

Look at traditional flower beds in parks and gardens with themes — commemorative flower beds etc. (e.g. those seen in seaside resorts.

Ask children to suggest a suitable space in the school grounds they can plan a garden for — preferably a piece of grassland that they can measure and lay out the final design.

Children then calculate the area of their planned bed, the perimeter of its border the measurements and layout of their design etc.

Leave the theme open ended: could be commemorative / decorative, for a special school or royal occasion, birth or wedding or just be decorative (the school logo?).

Will they make it symmetrical — if so how can they make sure it will be? How can they mark out circles, semi-circles, quarter-circles (quadrants)?

Give them the info tags of the colourful, low growing types of plants that are/were used in these types of flowerbeds (pansies, lobelia etc.).

Encourage them to look at the spread and draw scale plans of their design.

How many plants of each colour will fit their design?

How much will it cost to make?

Each group could make their design, using coloured circles of life-size dimensions to represent each plant and peg it in place through the centre using wire pegs (tent pegs or similar made from heavy florist wire) on the grass area.

Take photos before dismantling and then the next group make theirs, unless you have sufficient space for all groups to be working alongside each other.

NB It would be really great if one of the gardens to actually be made (a competition?) – perhaps sponsorship from a local garden centre could be sought? If you already have a garden club it could work with that too.

Learning Benefits:

- Active learning
- Real – life scenario – maths in the 'real world'
- Team-work
- Supports NC 2014 Programmes of Study for Maths
- Cross-curricular links – DT. History. Geography

****

Bird cakes

Numeracy Focus: *Measurement – standard and non-standard measures.*

Suitable for: KS1 in pairs

What you will need:

Per pair of children: a quarter cup of wild bird seed; a tablespoon of raisins; a quarter cup of lard at room temperature; measuring cups or spoons; rulers; yoghurt pots with a small hole in the bottom; string; scissors; mixing bowls; forks; trees, bird table or hook outside the classroom.

What you do:

(Check for children with allergies beforehand as bird feed will often contain peanuts.)

Give each pair a mixing bowl, measuring cups or spoons, a yoghurt pot and string.

Ask children to measure the string and cut it to a length of 40cms.

Tie a big knot in one end and thread it through the hole in the yoghurt pot.

Then ask them to measure a quarter cup of lard, a quarter cup of wild bird seed and a tablespoon of raisins.

Mix it together well until it is all held in by the lard – using their fingers if necessary.

Put it in the yoghurt pot and then place in the fridge for a couple of hours.

Hang them upside down on a nearby tree, bird table or hook – high enough so cats can't climb up and reach.

Learning Benefits:

- Active learning
- Real – life scenario
- Maths with a purpose
- Cross-curricular links - Science
- Supports NC 2014 Programmes of Study for Maths

****

Car Park Conundrums

Numeracy Focus: *Measurement – length, perimeter. Area. Volume. Problem Solving.*

Suitable for: Year 2 and KS2 in pairs or small groups.

What you will need:

Car park and clipboards; a selection of different measuring equipment including some 'less efficient' tools for children to choose from. (e.g. small rulers)

What you do:

Explain the task and ask children to choose which measuring equipment they would like to use.

Year 2 - Measure the length of the car park and the length of one car.

Year 3/4 – Measure the perimeter of a car parking space.

What is the total length of the lines in the car park?

Year 5/6 - Measure the area of a car park space.

What is the total area of the car park that cars can actually park in?

How much bigger is the whole area of the car park?

What is the space left over used for?

Could it be used more efficiently?

Problem Solving and Thinking:

Year 2 – How many cars the same length as the head teacher's would fit in the car park in a line? Are all cars the same length? Which type of car could we fit more of into the car park?

Year 3/4 - We would need 0.5 litres *(Change the amount of paint needed to make the calculation easier or harder)* of paint to do 10 metres of line, so how much paint would we need to paint the lines if we wanted to paint them again in a different colour?

Year 5 /6 - We want to add three more spaces to the car park – what area of land would we need?

How do you think the planners arrived at the size of each space as they did?

How much bigger than the area of the smallest car and the area of the largest car is each space?

If each square metre of car park needs 1.2 cubic metre of tarmac, how much more tarmac would we need if we wanted to make 3 more parking spaces?

Is it the best use of space – could it be used more efficiently /could you fit any more spaces into the area?

Can you work out what the turning circle of the car would be from the length and width of the car?

How much space is needed to drive in and out?

Imagine the head teacher wants to buy a big 4x4. Would s/he be able to park it in the car park and manoeuvre it in and out?

Learning Benefits:

- Active and real life problem solving
- Practical use of appropriate equipment for measuring longer things.
- Introduces and reinforces square and cubic measures, as well as perimeter
- Supports NC 2014 Programmes of Study for Maths

****

Car Park Data Collection

Numeracy Focus: *Statistics – collecting and recording data. Problem solving.*

Suitable for: KS1 and KS2 in pairs or small groups

What you will need: Car park to use; risk assessment; clipboards and writing materials.

What you do:

Year 2 – Predict which you think is the most popular colour for a car.

Record the colours of the cars in the car park using a tally chart.

Make a pictogram block graph to show the data.

What is the most common colour?

Were you right?

Year 3 – Record how often different numbers appear on the registration plates in the car park using a tally chart and make a bar chart.

What is the most common number?

How many times more /less does 0 appear than other numbers? etc.

Year 4 – Are people buying smaller cars these days? What would you predict to be the answer to that?

Measure and record the lengths of the vehicles on the car park using a tally chart.

Make a graph to show the data.

What is the difference in length between the longest and shortest cars?

What is the average length of car?

What space would we save if the car park spaces were made to fit each car exactly into the car park? Is that a practical idea?

Talk more about averages and their use.

Year 5/6 - What is likely to be the most popular type of car(s)?

Which would you like to buy if you could choose? Why?

In groups, children collect data about makes and models of cars in the car park.

Back in the classroom they can research each model to find the top speed and mpg.

Can they make a graph to show the top speed of each model or the fuel economy?

Can they find out which is the most economical car in the car park?

Which is the fastest car?

Can they make a line graph to show whether there is any correlation between fuel economy and top speed?

Which car would they choose?

Is it the same choice as before they carried out their research or have they changed their mind?

Learning Benefits:

- Real-life investigation
- Thinking about a range of issues that can affect purchases made
- Expressing an opinion based on a range of information
- Supports NC 2014 Programmes of Study for Math

****

Castles in the Sand

Numeracy Focus: *Measurement - estimating mass. Statistics – line graphs. Problem Solving.*

Suitable for: KS1 and KS2 – small groups

What you will need: Several bags of play sand; buckets of different sizes and spades; sand trays or builders trays; weighing scales.

What you do:

Give children all the equipment and one bag of sand.

Year 1 - Set them a challenge to work out how many sandcastles they can build from one bag. (Let them figure out that if they use a smaller bucket they get more castles)

How much water do they have to add to get the sand just right - to make stable sandcastles?

If they had 2 bags of sand, how many sandcastles could they make? Or if they had 3 bags?

Can they record their working out – e.g. use repeated addition?

Year 2 – As above. How much sand would they need to make a castle for each member of the class? Encourage multiplication skills.

Year 3 – Six members of the class need a sandcastle – what is the biggest sandcastle they can have using one bag of sand?

How much does one sandcastle weigh?

How much does the whole bag weigh?

Year 4 /5 /6 - Make the longest sand castle they can from one bag of sand – create a chart on which to record their findings.

(They have to work out whether a wider based bucket, which will usually have a greater height, is worth using when it uses up more sand. i.e. they need to work out that long and low will give them the longest castle).

How many bags of sand will they need to make their sandcastle cover a certain distance?

Year 6 – Back in the classroom, children could plot a line graph for the approximate volume of the bucket (or the weight of sand used for each bucket) and the length of the sandcastle.

What conclusions can they draw from the graph?

Learning Benefits:

- Active and fun problem solving
- Team- work
- Covers NC 2014 Programmes of Study for Maths

****

Days and Months

Numeracy Focus: *Measurement – language relating to days of the week and months of the year.*

Suitable for: KS1 - Year 1 in pairs or threes.

What you will need:

Washing line and pegs.

Cards with the names of the days of the week on the front and numbered in order on the back.

Cards with the names of the months of the year on with seasonal pictures – these could be ones the children have drawn on themselves and numbered in order on the back.

What you do:

The children order the cards accordingly and then check the backs of the cards to see if they are in the correct order.

Then they need to say the words out loud when they have finished.

If they need to 'cheat' by looking for the numbers on the back a few times at first as they put them in order, then they can, but eventually they have to do it without cheating.

They could go on to set trails for each other – hiding the cards and getting the other team to find them and order them in the quickest time.

Learning Benefits:

- Active learning
- Team-work
- Supports NC 2014 Programmes of Study for Maths

Divide and Conquer

Numeracy Focus: *Number – division, multiplication.*

Suitable for: KS1 and KS2. Whole class

What you will need:

Any large play space. Up to 12 PE mats, large hoops or long skipping ropes made into hoops. 2 coloured PE bands or bibs. Hand held white board and pen.

What you do:

KS1 intro - set out a number of mats or large hoops. Ask the children to make equal groups on the mats

Is anyone left over?   What does that mean?

Have we not shared properly or doesn't the number divide exactly?

What do we call the left overs?

What happens if we take away a mat and share again?

Can they think of a number sentence to explain what they did?

What is the starting number for the number sentence?

The game - you can use this just as a game or turn it into any type of 'goody vs. baddy' game for use in a creative curriculum – Pirates and Sailors, Knights and Dragons, Invaders etc.

When you explain how to play the game make sure that you ask questions that will provoke use of vocabulary such as multiple and factors – if this is new to your children from Year 3 up, then teach it now – the whole of the group who are free being the multiple and the hoops being one factor of that multiple – they have to find the other factor to keep safe.

Hoops are safe places or islands and the two 'chasers' (wearing the PE bands) need to catch their enemies.
You choose how many hoops to put out and write a division number sentence

on the white board appropriate to the on the group size and the number of hoops you have put out.

The children have to work out the answer to decide how many people can take refuge in each of the hoops and whether they need to launch a 'life raft' by asking you for an emergency hoop to save the 'remainders'.

Meanwhile, the 'chasers' have to work it out too and capture the correct remainder of children to walk the plank / put in their dungeon / keep in their lair etc.

If they think there will be no remainders they have to try to capture as many as they can before everyone else is safely in the hoops.

Rearrange the hoops and number sentence according to how many are left in the game each time. If at any time no-one is caught, then the captives are 'freed' or can 'escape' to play again. You can change the 'chasers' as and when you like.

Year 1 / 2 – 2, 5 and 10 mats or hoops

Year 3 – 3, 4 and 8 mats or hoops

Year 4 – 6 - up to 12 mats or hoops

Learning Benefits:

- Understand the relationship between multiplication and division in an active way
- Both the chasers and the chased have to work quickly as a team
- Opportunities to introduce and reinforce the vocabulary of multiplication and division
- Supports NC 2014 Programmes of Study for Maths
- Cross-curricular links – Themes

****

Double the Fun

Numeracy Focus: *Number - multiplication*

Suitable for: KS1

What you will need:

Teams of 3 or 4 children; enough seed trays / boxes for each team; outdoor space with plenty of stones, gravel or sticks (they will be replaced!)

What you do:

Ask each team to place 1 item in their box.

Then explain that they need to double the number of items in their box each time by running and finding more items.

The first team to double their number gets a point.

Stop in between each 'doubling', count the items in each box and take a moment to all repeat the number sentence e.g. 'double 1 is 2' (1 x 2 = 2).

Initially, work through the numbers in order by removing items from each box after you have counted them.

For example, after they have made 'double 2 is 4', remove 1 item so they can make double 3 the next time.

Scatter the items back so they can collect them again if necessary.

At the end of the session, see if they can recall the answers to the doubling number sentences that they have done.

Follow it up in the classroom by talking about how we write number sentences with doubling and make the links to counting in 2's.

For Year 2, use it to introduce the two times table.

Perhaps you could take photos of the boxes they used, with the items in to remind them of the answers they need at a later date.

Learning Benefits:

- Active and fun
- Saying the number sentence reinforces the vocabulary
- Team-work
- Supports NC Programmes of Study in Maths

****

Everything in Order?

Numeracy Focus: Ordering numbers or objects.

Suitable for: KS1 and lower KS2 - pairs

What you will need:

Year 1 - Washing line and pegs; number cards 1-20; picture cards or real objects which can be pegged up – e.g. different sized tshirts or socks etc.

Year 2 – large number cards 1-100; clip on identity tags with random numbers 1-100.

Year 3 – Clip on identity tags with random numbers 1-1000.

Year 4 - Clip on identity tags with random numbers over 1000.

What you do:

Year 1 / 2 - Give the children the number cards or objects you want them to order and ask them to peg them up.

Year 2 / 3 / 4 – give the children an identity card and get them to order themselves.

Learning Benefits:

- Active learning
- Team-work
- Supports NC 2014 Programmes of Study for Maths

****

Fee Fi Foe Fum

– could you outrun the giant?

Numeracy Focus: *Measurement - length and time. Problem Solving*

Suitable for: KS1 – small groups

What you will need:

Playground/outdoor space; children in pairs; 2 cardboard cut-outs of a giant footprint (about a metre long) – 1 per group; measuring tapes; trundle wheels & other measuring equipment; stop watches; clipboards; pencils and paper.

What you do:

Year 1/2 –

Ask the children 'How we could find out how many strides it would take for the giant to cross the playground by using his footprint?'

How many do they think?

Get them to check their stride compared to their foot size – is it double or more?

What length do they estimate the Giant's stride would be to the nearest metre – can they measure?

How long is the playground?

How many Giant strides will it take?

Year 2 – Giants aren't good at running and they walk at one stride per second - how long will it take him to cross the playground?

In pairs, get the children to time themselves to see how fast they can run the length of the playground and record their results.

Could they beat him?

Learning Benefits:

- Fun and active maths
- Health benefits
- Supports NC 2014 Programmes of Study in Maths
- Cross-curricular links - PE / Literacy (Jack and the Beanstalk)

****

Find the Fractions

Numeracy Focus: *Fractions. Decimals. Improper fractions.*

Suitable for: KS1 and KS2

What you will need: Large play space with hiding places.

Year 1 – Large squares, rectangles, circles of different sizes divided into halves; squares, rectangles and circles divided into quarters; stopwatch.

Year 2 – as above but divided into thirds as well.

Year 3 – as above but divided into different numbers, including tenths.

Year 3/4 – Pairs of number cards with fractions written on in tenths or hundredths which add to a whole (enough for 6 per team) or tenth fractions cards and their decimal equivalents (enough for 6 per team).

Year 5 – Make 6 cards for each team with denominators that are multiples of the same number - make them different for each team.

Year 6 – improper fraction bingo cards (different for each team) and/or matching whole number/fraction cards.

For example:

$^{14}/_5$	
$^{26}/_9$	
$^{17}/_3$	
$^{32}/_{10}$	

What you do:

Year 1 / 2 – Hide the fractions of shapes in the play space. Half the class are finders and the other half are the makers. When they find a piece the finders bring it back to the makers who have to try to make the whole shapes as quickly as they can.

Time them and then swap over. Hide the pieces again and see if they can beat their time.

Alternatively, if you make enough shapes you could split them into teams and each team could have the same fractions of shapes in a pile to make into whole shapes. The first team to finish wins.

Year 3 – Find and match the shapes as above to make whole shapes.

Year 3 / 4 – Divide the class into small teams and hide one half of the different pairs of 10ths or 100ths which add to make a whole and share out the remaining halves between the teams.

Quickest team to find the pairs win.

Year 4 - Hide the decimal equivalents cards and share out the tenths cards between the teams. Again, quickest to find the equivalent decimals for their fractions win.

Year 5 – Hide 5 cards from each set around the play space and give each team their remaining card. They have to find the other five cards in their set and when they have collected them all put them in order. Quickest team wins.

Children can then hide 5 of their cards and swap over the remaining card with the other teams and play again.

Year 6 – Hide whole number and fraction cards in the play space and give each team a set of improper fraction cards. The teams have to find the whole number cards and fraction cards that add to equal the improper fractions.

Example: they have the improper fraction card $^{14}/_5$ and they have to find the cards 2 and $^4/_5$. The team who match them correctly and the quickest wins.

Children then all hide the cards around the play space, swap bingo cards, and play again.

Learning Benefits:

- Active learning
- Team-work
- Supports NC 2014 Programmes of Study for Maths

****

Find Your Way Home

Numeracy Focus: *Geometry - position and direction. Problem solving.*

Suitable for: KS1 and KS2 in pairs.

What you will need: Large play space; various pieces of PE equipment e.g. 'A' frames, cones, skipping ropes, beanbags, mats etc.; large pieces of fabric to represent water; blindfolds for half the children in the group; cards with different '**Starting Points**' and '**Home Destinations**' written on.

What you do:

This can be made to fit in with many different themes (A Pirates Treasure Map / Town map / Outer Space etc.) but for the purpose of explaining the activity, we are aliens finding our way home in outer space.

Make a 3D map with the PE equipment and put signs on the various pieces - Earth, the Moon, Jupiter, Mars and Venus etc.

Give each pair a '**Starting Point - Destination**' card – i.e. each pair starts at a different planet and works their way around the 'map' using different routes – ending up at their own 'Destination'.

One child is blindfolded and is guided by their partner who can only use the vocabulary of direction and position.

They must estimate the number of paces it will take their partner to move to their next place. (no hand holding or physical guiding).

Encourage the use of vocabulary appropriate for each year group.

Year 1 – right, left, forward, backward, quarter-turn, half-turn.

Year 2/3/4 – North, South, East and West. NW, NE, SW, SE, right angle, clockwise, anticlockwise.

Year 5/6 – As above. Describe the angle of turn needed to travel more efficiently to take the shortest route to each place.

Taking it further:

Extend the cards with different places the alien has to visit on the way home. Have a points system for each place successfully visited.

Mark scores on their card as the pair guide each other around the 'map'.

Learning Benefits:

- Fun and active maths
- Team work
- Supports the NC 2014 Programmes of Study
- Cross-curricular links - Geography

****

Frivolous Fractions

Numeracy Focus: *Number - equivalent fractions, decimals and percentages. Measurement - length and volume.*

Suitable for: Upper KS2 in groups.

What you will need: A large area with access to natural things to collect. Alternatively, scatter manmade items around the space.

0.2	20%	¹/₅
0.8	80%	⁴/₅

0.5	50%	½
0.8	80%	⁴/₅

0.5	50%	½
0.25	25%	¼

0.4	40%	²/₅
0.5	50%	½

0.25	25%	¼
0.4	40%	²/₅

0.2	20%	¹/₅
0.4	40%	²/₅

6 large A3 boards, marked as above (if laminated they can be re-used).

Six sets of 6 playing cards which match the boards – you could colour code them for ease of sorting and make an answer card for quick checking of their calculations; a jug for each group; a metre of string for each group; metre sticks with centimetres marked on; beanbags or similar.

What you do:

Write some 'commands' on the playing cards (examples below)

Collect $^1/_2$ of 20 stones
Fetch 50% of 10 fallen leaves
Take 0.5 of 14 beanbags
Fetch ¼litre of water
Cut 0.25 of a metre of string
Pick 25% of 12 blades of grass

The challenge is to be the first to fill their collector cards with the correct number, amount or length of objects.

Learning Benefits:

- Active learning
- Teamwork
- Healthy competition
- Supports NC 2014 Programmes of Study for Maths

****

Fuelled up

Numeracy Focus: *Measurement – capacity. Number - multiplication and division.*

Suitable for: Upper KS2

What you will need: Paddling pool (empty); one imperial and several metric measuring jugs; water; calculators; writing equipment.

What you do:

Talk about the cost of petrol and diesel and the amounts displayed on the big signs at petrol stations. What do they mean?

Discuss what other liquids are sold by the litre (Bottled water, orange juice, milk etc.).

Which do they think is the most expensive? (e.g. compare a litre of bottled water with petrol).

Car petrol tank capacity is measured in litres. Let the children see the size of a car petrol tank by getting them to fill up the paddling pool with 50 litres of water (an average sized tank).

Discuss how we work out how economical a car is; mpg = miles per gallon.

Explain that gallon is an imperial measure – do they know any other imperial measures? Talk about imperial measures for capacity being in fluid ounces, pints and gallons.

Have they heard or seen those words before? Where? Talk about whether metric is easier to calculate and why.

To work out how much our fuel is costing we still need to convert from gallons to litres and vice versa. Tell them that there are 20 fluid ounces (fl.oz) in a British pint and 8 pints in a gallon.

Using the measuring jugs and water, can they work out how many fluid ounces make a litre? (35.195 fl.oz) Conversely, how many millilitres make a pint? (568.261ml)

Using this information how can we work out how many miles our car will drive on one litre of petrol, if the manufacturer says it will do 50mpg?

How many miles will it do to a tank?

How much will it cost per mile?

Example:

Per litre petrol costs = £1.40

Litres in a gallon = 4.546

Per gallon petrol costs = £1.40 x 4.546 litres = £6.364

50 mpg so therefore £6.364÷50 = 0.127 rounded to 13p per mile

£1.40 ÷ 13 = 10.769 miles per litre

Learning Benefits:

- Active learning
- Real – life objects and scenario
- Investigating
- Team-work
- Supports NC 2014 Programmes of Study for Maths

****

Funfair

Numeracy Focus: *Measurement – money. Number - addition; subtraction. Problem solving.*

Suitable for: KS1 and KS2

What you will need:

Money – play or real (don't forget to put systems in place to get it returned); 3 beanbags; a target for the floor; goal posts or improvised goal posts; 1 coconut, cone; large ball; skittles; ball (or a hockey puck if on grass - to throw instead of roll); 3 hoops and a cone.

What you do:

Set up five activities around the play area. The activities could be **Hoopla** (with a cone and hoops) **Beat the Goalie, Bulls-eye** (target on the floor and throw beanbags), **Coconut Shy** (one coconut sitting on the top of a cone and 3 balls) **Ten Pin bowling** (Skittles and large ball).

Each activity has a stall holder to take the money and an assistant to set up the equipment each time. This means that you will have just over half the class as visitors to begin with.

Each activity needs to cost a different amount and in denominations that you choose, according to ability. Give every child an appropriate amount of money to play with. The children are allowed 3 goes at each activity.

Year 1 - Use exact denominations to pay so that they just have to find the correct coin.

Year 2 – Use amounts so they have to combine coins to make the total needed (depending on ability). To extend, give out coins that will need change.

Year 3/4 – Make the cost of the activity £ and pence, rounded to the nearest 10p and give them coins or notes so that will need change.

Year 5/6 – Give one note and make the cost of the activities in £ and pence, not rounded to the nearest 10p.

The prize for 3 out of three hits, strikes or goals is their money back.

Make the cost of the activity an even amount so that the prize for 2 out of 3 can be half their money back. For 1 out of three make it a denomination of coin related to the original cost.

You can play this throughout the year extending it each time according to where the children are at. Make a price list and prize boards as you would get at a fair – re-use them in the future and just stick labels over the previous amounts.

Example:

```
                    Hoopla

   3 hoops for 10p

   3 Hits - your money back

   2 Hits - half your money back

   1 Hit - 2p
```

Swap over half way through the session so they all get a turn to use money either as a visitor or as a stall holder.

Some children may finish a lot earlier than half way through and have no money left. You may want to give the children extra goes to keep them busy but they can't win any prize money if they don't pay!

At the end of the session the children can work out whether they made any money and how much they actually spent including the prize money they may have won.

Ask children to work out which half of the class (when they swapped into visitor role) was most successful.

Learning Benefits:

- Real life scenario makes it relevant
- Problem solving - working out what they can afford/ how many goes to have.
- Cross-curricular links – PE (the physical activity/ eye-hand coordination)
- Both the stallholders and visitors have to mentally work out money problems
- Supports NC 2014 Programmes of Study for Math

****

Get Together

Numeracy Focus: *Number - facts to 10, to 20, 100. Multiplication. Problem Solving*

Suitable for: KS1 and KS2

What you will need:

Clip on identity tags (self-adhesive or laminated for which you can either make permanent number cards or the ones with flaps so you can change the numbers throughout the year).

Alternatively, for a one off game you could use numbered sticky labels.

What you do:

Make number badges for the numbers appropriate to the ability of your children.

The task is to run around the outdoor space and when the adult shouts a number, the children get together to make that number.

Year 1 - number tags 0-5 several times – e.g. find a partner to make ten.

Year 2 - number tags 0-5 several times – make ten with more than one number.

Year 3/4 - number tags 0-5 - make small numbers below 100 using any operation they like and using as many numbers as they like.

They must try to use everyone in the class.

Can they rearrange themselves to use everyone?

Years 5/6 - number tags – you can choose any six numbers up to 12 on the tags several times over.

Give the class a large number and get them to make that number by getting together and using any operation.

For example;

If you give tags 3-8 several times over and ask them to find 48, they may decide – 6x8 / 7x5+5+8 / 3x4x4 / 8x8-6-5-5 etc. etc.

If some are left without a group, line them up and get the whole class to suggest combinations that can be made.

Learning Benefits:

- Active learning
- Supports NC 2014 Programmes of Study for Maths

****

Go the Extra Mile

Numeracy Focus: *Measurement - length. Problem Solving.*

Suitable for: Upper KS2

What you will need:

Drive a mile in different directions around your school to pick the best route for an outing with your class.

When you have chosen, drive a kilometre (0.621 of a mile) back from the end point and note the spot.

Sufficient adult to child ratio for the size of your group; water bottles; snack for the destination (optional, but they'll love it!); a timing device.

What you do:

Ask the children if they have any idea how far a mile is.

If they walked from the school, where do they think they would end up?

How long would it take? Ask them to make a note of what they say.

How else can we measure distance?

What is the difference between a kilometre and a mile?

Which is further?

Take your class as a whole or in small groups for a walk along the route to the mile point.

Time how long it takes and if any of them have watches, ask them to time it too.

Stop and have drinks and a snack.

Was it further or nearer than they thought?   How long did it take?

On the way back stop at the one kilometre point?

How far are they away from the school?

Do they estimate they are less than halfway? Over halfway?

How long did it take?

How much longer do they think it will take to get back?

Back at school you can continue with the discussion and practise some conversions of distances to solve problems.

As we still use both miles and kilometres in this country, there are lots of real-life scenarios where someone may need to convert miles to kms.

For example; 'Your parents are taking you to Disneyland Paris and they need to make sure they know the speed limits on the roads but French speed limits are in km/hour.

How could you help them?

Work out the speed limit in km for 50 miles/hour.

Learning Benefits:

- Active learning
- Real – life scenarios
- Health benefits
- Cross-curricular links – Geography (local area)
- Supports NC 2014 Programmes of Study for Maths

****

Gridlock

Numeracy Focus: *Geometry - Position and Direction.*

Suitable for: Year 4 - whole class

What you will need:

Playground Chalk; coordinate cards - large and laminated; stopwatch.

What you do:

Before the lesson, mark a large 4 x 5 grid on the playground - the x axis needs to be spaced wide enough for the children to get past each other.

Explain what co-ordinates are used for.

Number the axes whilst the children are watching and explain each axis.

Children line up at 0 ready to walk along the x axis and up the y axis one at a time.

Give each child a co-ordinate card.

They need to find their places on the grid as quickly as possible.

To check they are all in the right place, get each row to hold up their cards, when they have all finished.

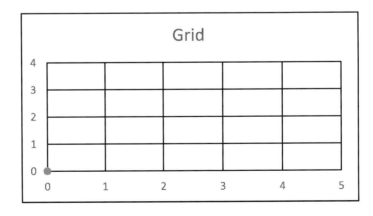

Make sure they stand on the co-ordinate points and not in the square.

Swap cards and try again using a stopwatch to see if they can improve the time it takes.

Ask children to think of coordinates for each other – working in pairs.

They could place 'treasure' on a couple of points on the gird and ask another pair to write the coordinates down.

Learning Benefits:

- Active learning
- Supports NC 2014 Programmes of Study for Maths
- Cross-curricular links - Geography

****

Guess the Weight of the...

Numeracy Focus: *Measurement – mass.*

Suitable for: KS2

What you will need:

4 or 5 sets of 6 everyday items, wrapped in brown paper (that weigh different amounts) – e.g. flour, sugar, can of beans etc.; laminated cards with the corresponding weights in grams written on;

For *year 5/6* - extra cards to write on; calculators.

What you do:

Give each team a set of items.

The idea of the game is to be the first team to estimate the weights of all the individual items and match them with the corresponding card.

It could be a running task, (a PE activity) or the cards could be hidden in a tray of bran or shaving foam to make it more of a challenge/game.

Year 4 - As a team they must estimate the weight of the first item and send the first person in the team to collect the corresponding card.

Year 5 – As above but they also have to convert each mass in grams into kg and make a new card for each item.

Year 6 – Use the same sets of items but have the cards to match in pounds and ounces.

Ask children to convert their estimates using the conversion 1kg =2.2lbs and collect the correct card.

Learning Benefits:

- Active learning
- Team-work
- Real-life objects
- Supports NC 2014 Programmes of Study for Maths

****

Hang it Out

Numeracy Focus: *Number - sequences.*

Suitable for: KS1 and KS2 – whole class in mixed ability pairs or small groups if you have a large class

What you will need:

Large outdoor space; A4 paper (you could cut them into t-shirt or sock shapes!); marker pens; washing line or thick string and pegs; playground line marking or long skipping rope; cones.

What you do:

String up a washing line across the play space low enough for your smallest child to reach.

Children work in pairs with several sheets of paper and a marker pen.

Tell them they are going to work out sequences of numbers - each with the same operation (or operations depending on ability) in between each number – what we call 'the rule'.

Examples:

Year 2 +2 / +5 /+10
Year 3 +3 / +4 / x2
Year 4 x2 +1 / +25
Year 5 +6 ÷2 / square numbers / prime numbers / decimals
Year 6 all of the above – make the starting number negative

Show them the line behind which you want them to stand, so they don't all edge forward to the sequence washing line.

Make sure the washing line is sited far enough away to run to but close enough to see the answers when pegged on. One partner will scribe (make sure they know to write it as big as they can) and the other will be the runner who will peg the answer on the line.

Give the children the rule and a start number.

Each pair or small group works out the answer and when they have scribed it, the runner races to the washing line – it's a good idea to position someone here to adjudicate who is first and second.

The answer is pegged on the line and the rest of the children check whether it is correct.

If incorrect, the one who was second pegs up their number and has it checked by the class.

The pair or group who find the most numbers in the sequence wins.

Taking it further:

Give a higher starting number and do subtraction sequences.

Make the calculation more complicated and include a division element.

Start from a variety of numbers including 100's and 1000's depending on ability.

Learning Benefits:

- All remain active because they have a job to perform
- All need to check the answer is correct
- Healthy competition
- Paired / team work
- The washing line makes the sequence visual

****

Hide and Seek

Numeracy Focus: *Number facts to 20 (can also be done with number facts to 10)*

Suitable for: KS1 and early KS2 (for consolidation). Whole class or groups.

What you will need:

Any large outdoor space; number cards 1-20 (double up some of the cards for a group larger than 20); white boards and pens.

What you do:

Give out cards 0-10 to half the group (or several sets of 0-5 if you are working with bonds to 10).

These children then go and hide with their cards around the space whilst the others look away.

Give the remaining children the cards from 11-20. They need to go and find their number pair that makes 20. (or 10).

The children hiding must show their card when they are found and if they are part of the correct pair they race back to the adult together.

If they are not correct they continue hiding and the other continues searching.

When they are all back, swap the cards round and hide again.

Taking it further / Problem Solving and Thinking:

When they return, can the children write out the number facts for their numbers and 20 on their white boards?

To keep them busy while the others are being found ask them to think of some other number bonds that make 20, so they know which numbers to look for next time.

Learning Benefits:

- Actively learning
- Both the 'seeker' and the 'hider' have to work out whether they make the correct total
- Supports NC 2014 Programmes of Study for Maths

****

Hot or Cold?

Numeracy Focus: *Measurement – temperature. Statistics – collecting and recording data in line graphs. Number.*

Suitable for: KS1 and KS2

What you will need: Outside thermometer.

What you do:

All Year Groups - Ask children to read the temperature outside at the same time every day on a regular basis.

Use the Celsius scale.

Don't forget to use the correct vocabulary from the start – degrees / Celsius / thermometer etc. This could be part of the daily routine, year round.

Year 1 – Using Celsius means that the numbers will be accessible for most children in this age group and will give them practice recording the numbers themselves.

They can see whether the numbers are higher or lower than the day before.

Year 2/3 – As above: familiarisation with reading scales and comparing data over time.

Year 4 - Collect data about the temperature outside over time and use to make time graphs – make sure they have all had a turn at reading the thermometer a couple of times.

Year 5 – As they are collecting their data about outside temperatures they can start recording it in both Celsius and Fahrenheit.

Also talk about body thermometers and compare the different scales on them.

The two scales are both used and they should be aware that 100°C is vastly different to 100°F, so we need to know which measure we are using to save an unnecessary trip to the hospital!

Talk about the general conversion for body temperature – 37°C = 98.6

Year 6 – Collect the charts over time and when they have a few months' worth of data they can work out the mean temperatures and record them in a line graph.

Learning Benefits:

- Active learning
- Real – life maths with a purpose
- Supports NC 2014 Programmes of Study for Maths

****

I Spy Shapes

Numeracy Focus: *Geometry - shape recognition*

Suitable for: KS1 and KS2

What you will need:

Any outdoor space, preferably where the children can also see buildings and structures; stop watch; digital cameras; sketch book; pencils (optional).

What you do:

Give the children a specific time limit to find as many different shapes as they can (this will depend on the area you wish them to cover and the amount of shapes you think they should be able to find).

Let them take pictures with a digital camera or a sketch book to capture the shapes they find.

Year 1 - circle / square / triangle / rectangle / hexagon / pentagon (for differentiation for less able children, give a list or pictures of the shapes you want them to find).

Year 2 - circle / square / triangle / rectangle / hexagon / pentagon / octagon - - ask them to find shapes with 1 or 2 lines of symmetry

Year 3 - diamond / kite / cube / cuboid / pyramid / sphere / cylinder /

Year 4 - right-angle triangle / isosceles triangle / scalene triangle / equilateral triangle / parallelogram / trapezium / rhombus

Year 5 /6 – all of the above

Taking it further /Problem Solving / Thinking:

Ask them to find 3D shapes - cylinder / pyramid / cube / cuboid / cone / sphere prisms / other polyhedrons – can they count the faces and name them?

Children could make a display or PowerPoint of their pictures to present their findings to the class.

Learning Benefits:

- Active maths
- Maths in the real world
- Supports NC 2014 Programmes of Study
- Cross-curricular links - ICT

****

Ladders

Numeracy Focus: *Number facts - doubles, halves, odd and even, multiples.*

Suitable for: KS1 and KS2. Whole class.

What you will need:

Any large outdoor space; A4 laminated numbers (bespoke to your objective and year group)

What you do:

Ask children to get into pairs and sit opposite each other with their toes touching, so that you make a ladder with enough space in between for children to run and step over each 'rung' of legs.

NB* It is really important that they keep their legs straight and still. If they are too young or particularly 'wriggly', you could always use skipping ropes between the pairs and they could sit with legs folded.

Each side of the ladder is a team and can be given a name.

Year 1 and 2

Numeral recognition - use the game in its age-old format, numbering each team with any set of consecutive numbers (or all even numbers or all odd numbers).

Hold up the number cards rather than shouting them out so the children have to remain attentive and recognise their own number.

When children recognise their own number they race their pair from the other team up the ladder, down the outside of the ladder and back up the inside to their place.

The one who sits down first gets a point for their team.

Number facts – For number facts to 10 you only need 22 children so give any children left over a chance to record the point and adjudicate and then swap them in later.

Number each pair of children and ask them to remember their number. Tell the children they must make pairs of numbers that add to 10 so that two pairs of children will be racing at the same time.

Shout out a number. That pair and the 'matching pair' that will make the total to ten have to race up the ladder and down the sides and back up the ladder to their places. The team who are both sat down first get the point.

Year 2 onwards

Halving – Number each pair from 1 to however many pairs you have. Shout out an appropriate number double and the pair who together make that number race each other up the ladder, down the side and back up the ladder to their places. The one who sits down first gets a point for their team. Swap them about and re-number so that they practise other doubles.

Make it harder by numbering your teams with larger numbers.

Doubling – as above but number each pair with a number double and shout out numbers which are half.

Multiples – Number each line in the appropriate multiples for the year group e.g. number Year 2's in twos, fives or tens and shout out an appropriate times table question. When they work out that they are the answer they race each other up and down the ladder as above.

Learning Benefits:

- Healthy team competition
- No-one can fail because they will be helped and 'nudged' by their team
- Aids memorisation in an active way
- Health benefits
- Supports NC 2014 Programmes of Study for Maths

****

Let's Go Fly a Kite

Numeracy Focus: *Geometry - shape and angles. Measurement – length. Statistics - record data. Problem solving.*

Suitable for: KS2 – working in pairs

What you will need:

A breezy day!; crepe paper ; thin dowelling; tape; protractors; set squares; stop watches.

What you do:

You can decide how easy or detailed you want this activity to be, depending on whether you are linking it to DT programmes of study and which particular maths objectives you want to focus on.

To make successful kites children need to make sure their dowelling is measured correctly and taped ***perpendicular*** to each other where they cross over - making four ***right angles*** around the cross over point.

(***Year 3s*** could use a ***set square*** to check and ***Year 4 onwards measure*** these angles with a ***protractor)***

(The sail can be made from crepe paper - make sure the points of the dowel are taped down well.)

Key thinking questions might include:

How long does the string need to be?

Is there a 'best' length of string for the most successful flying?

Whose flies for the longest time?

Record the data.

How could we work out whose kite is flying the highest?

Does the shape of the kite make a difference?

Is a wider or slimmer kite more successful? Why might that be?

Learning Benefits:

- Maths with a purpose
- Active learning
- Cross-curricular links – Science. DT
- Supports NC 2014 Programmes of Study for Maths

****

Let's grow

Numeracy Focus: *Measure - length, area and perimeter. Problem Solving.*

Suitable for: KS1 and lower KS2 – pairs or small groups to plan / whole class project to execute.

What you will need:

Information tags from flowering plants and vegetables. These can be real or researched from the internet and made into tags. (choose plants that will grow to different heights.) If you have some real plants as examples in school even better; garden canes; paper; a laminator.

What you do:

The task is to plan a border or section of an allotment for the school grounds. They will need to measure the area and then decide which plants to plant where, according to the plants height and spread.

Will they mix vegetables and flowers? If so which ones.

If this is not an actual real-life task then the children can make life size plants by using their measuring skills for the correct height and measure the distance between them when they 'plant' them in the grass area.

Year 1 – Show children the area they are going to design for. Ask the children to measure the height and spread (width and depth) of real examples, if you have them, and then look at info tags of other plants to see if they can identify the same measurements on the tags.

Give them templates of the plants that you have chosen for them to use and get them to estimate how many will fit in their area.

They then try it out and see how good their estimate was.

Ask them to draw a simple bird's eye view plan using symbols for the different types of plants (could be different shapes or colour coded circles).

Challenge some children to have a 'graded effect' - with the tallest plants at the back and the shortest at the front.

Use the best plan and challenge the children to make the plants by drawing or painting the flowers or fruit they produce.

Cut them out and laminate them.

Ask children to measure and cut / hacksaw garden canes to the correct length for their plant.

Each child then puts their flower or vegetable in the correct place in the garden following the plan. Take a photo.

Year 2 – As above and children use the tags to compare and order the heights of the plants – find the tallest and the widest. Use <> and = to record their ordering.

Year 3/4 – As above and children use the spread measurement to make a square so they can check how many plants will fit into the area. How will they make sure their squares have right angles?

Learning Benefits:

- Team work
- Maths with a purpose
- Cross-curricular links – Design, Literacy, History. Geography (Maps and plans)
- Supports NC 2014 Programmes of Study for Maths

****

Logistics

Numeracy Focus: *Measurement - volume and mass. Algebra. Problem Solving*

Suitable for: Upper KS2

What you will need:

Lots of large packing boxes preferably all the same size, flat packed; parcel tape; long tape measures or trundle wheels; pictures of removal lorries in different sizes.

What you do:

Before the lesson, mark out the area of a large lorry on the playground.

Width	2.26m
Height	2.18m
Length	5.94m

Also, have a long pole or piece of wood of just over 2m to demonstrate the height.

Tell the children that someone you know is moving but they don't know what size lorry they need. Show them pictures of removal lorries. How would we know which size to order if we wanted to move? Hopefully, they will come up with needing to know how much it holds (capacity) and how much 'stuff' there is (volume).

Show them one of the boxes. How do we measure how much space it takes up? Can they remember the equation for area of a rectangle? Area = a (length) x b (width)

Can they think what new dimension is added when you have a cuboid / rectangular prism and want to know how much space it would take up in the lorry? Can they guess at the equation? Volume = a (length) x b (width) x c (height)

Give each group a box and ask them to work out the volume. Share the results – are they all the same?

How many boxes we could fit in the lorry? Show them the lorry's area on the playground and tell them the height. Can they estimate how many boxes would fit into the lorry using their box as a guide?

Let them work it out in metric measures and then compare answers from the teams. Talk about how we record it as cubic metres m³ because of the 3 dimensions hence 3D shape.

Back in the classroom you then wonder whether that size of lorry will be big enough for all your stuff. Pull out the information below from your handbag or wallet and tell them the cubic feet that your furniture and belongings are estimated to take up. You could display it on a visualizer or have scanned it so you can display it on the IWB. Do they notice that the estimate is in cubic feet? How can we compare the two now?

Get them to convert their answer using the formula $1m^3 = 35.315ft^3$

Average figures for size of transport needed for moving home:

Student move= up to 200 cubic feet ~ Suitable vehicle = Transporter or Small Transit van

Studio Flat = 200 – 400 cubic feet ~ Suitable vehicle = Transit Van (Small or medium wheel base)

One bedroom Flat/house = 300 – 500 cubic feet ~ Suitable vehicle = Large Transit Van or Luton Van

Two Bedrooms Flat/house = 600 – 900 cubic feet ~ Suitable vehicle = Luton Van (3.5 T) or Small Truck (7.5)

Three Bedroom Flat/House = 800 – 1600 cubic feet ~ Suitable vehicle = Moving Truck 7.5 T

Learning Benefits:

- Active learning
- Real – life objects and scenario
- Investigation
- Team work
- Supports NC 2014 Programmes of Study for Maths

Make a Bolt for it

Numeracy Focus: *Measurement – length. Ratio and Proportion.*

Statistics – line graphs.

Suitable for: Upper KS2

What you will need: Playground or field; children in pairs; measuring tapes; trundle wheels etc. stop watches; large version of class chart like the one below - large poster size and A4 size copies.

What you do:

Begin by getting pairs of children to measure their height and record it on a whole class chart. (This could eventually be transferred to an interactive whiteboard). Get them to order the class from the shortest to the tallest.

Split the class into groups of 4 according to their height and ask them to time each other racing over 100m (or 50m if you don't have room) and record the result.

Next, ask them to measure the natural stride length of each member of their group (heel to heel).

Share all the results with the rest of the class (via the whiteboard perhaps at this point) - so every pair has all the results and then add shoe sizes to complete the chart.

Name	Height	100m speed	Stride length	Shoe size

Show them a video clip of a top athlete (Usain Bolt) running the 100m in the 2012 Olympics. See if they can identify what made him successful.

Thinking questions:

What is the ratio of shoe size to stride length?

Does height affect your shoe size?

As a class discuss the results on the chart – do they notice whether height, shoe size or stride length has an effect on the speed over 100m?

Can they choose one of the elements that they think has an effect on running speed and make a line graph of their results to try to prove it?

What could they do to improve their running performance?

Let them try to improve on their times.

Record the results to compare.

Learning Benefits:

- Fun and active learning
- Maths with a purpose
- Real – life scenario
- Supports NC 2014 Programmes of Study for Maths
- Cross-curricular links – PE / PHSE / Science.

****

Make a Mint

Numeracy Focus: *Measurement – money. Number - place value. Problem Solving.*

Suitable for: Year 2 and KS2 – whole class in 4 mixed ability groups.

What you will need:

PE equipment; 4 sets of laminated pictures of coins and notes (vary the size and extent of the set according to ability); optional - 4 sets of laminated cards with monetary values of £100, £10 (some with units of pence as well) or just pence in 10s and units according to ability; handheld whiteboard and pen.

What you do:

Set up an assault course with available PE equipment.

Divide the class into four mixed ability teams.

Hold up the whiteboard with an appropriate monetary value on it for all to see.

A member from all four teams has to go over the assault course and bring back one coin or note.

Each child adds what they bring back to the team total which must add up to value you have stated.

The first team to make the value is awarded points. Repeat as often as needed.

You could amend the challenge: e.g. get the full amount but in the least amount of coins / most amounts of coins / a coin that you would get change from i.e.10p etc. The team can discuss it before the team member does the assault course.

You can ask starter questions for specific children, according to ability:

- Find the amount that you need to exactly make 0.90
- Find the amount that is ten pounds more than £34.
- Find the amount that is 10p less than 60p etc.

Year 1 – You could start by asking recognition questions such as 'Find the 20p coin' or ask them to find the coin that is worth 10 pennies etc.

The first child back wins points for their team – if they get back and the team think it is wrong they can go back and change it.

Use values that will make simple additions with small value coins.

(As well as holding up the white board with the amount on it you may need to say it as well.)

Year 2 – Make values commensurate with their arithmetic ability. Coins up to £2.

Year 3 – Values commensurate with their arithmetic ability. All coins and notes.

Year 4 – All coins and values.

Year 5 – Up to £50 notes and larger monetary values including pence.

Year 6 – As above but extend to give them values in euros and ask them to convert to sterling first (using a calculator) – they have to get the right amount correctly rounded.

Give them euro coins and get them to convert the sterling value

<u>Learning Benefits:</u>

- Team work – collective thinking
- Real-life scenario
- Active learning
- Supports NC 2014 Programmes of Study for Maths

****

Mass

Numeracy Focus: *Measurement – mass. Using notation for greater than /less than.*

Suitable for: KS1 and lower KS2 – whole class in small groups.

What you will need:

An area to work where there are plenty of rocks and stones.

(If your school grounds don't have many you may want to think about enriching your environment by buying some in from the local builders' yard.)

Try adding some pumice stones to demonstrate bigger is not always heavier.

Year 1 - balance scales *Year 2 /3/4-* weighing scales; weight cards and 5 blank card labels for each group.

What to do:

Year 1 - Find 6 stones in the local environment and use balance scales to place them in order - heaviest to lightest.

Year 2 – As a group find 5 natural objects that weigh; (<50g)   (50g<100g) (exactly 100g)   (100g<200g)   (>1kg)

Make card labels to say how much they weigh.

Year 3/4 – As a group find an object that weighs 100g.

Now individually find something twice as heavy by estimating and bring it back to weigh – nearest estimate in the group wins.

As a group find something twice as heavy again – discuss and agree.

Weigh it to check.

Ask all children to think about when they might need to use their skills to estimate mass in everyday life.

Learning Benefits:

- Active learning
- Team work
- Supports NC 2014 Programmes of Study for Maths

****

Match Box Competition

Numeracy Focus: *Four operations of number fractions. Percentages. Statistics - data collection and recording. Problem solving.*

Suitable for: KS1 and KS2

What you will need: outside space; empty match boxes (or other small boxes that are all the same size) for each pair of children; visualizer (optional).

What you do:

This is a competition is to see how many different objects can be fitted into the match box. The objects must be whole things and each one different – so no bits of leaf torn up and stuffed in! Children go outside in pairs and find as many as they can fit in. Give them a specific length of time.

Year 1 – When it is full they come back to the class room and count their items. They could then tape them onto a piece of card. The pair with the most items wins. If you have a visualizer you could put them on to that and all count together. How did the winner get the most objects in the box – did they arrange them or just squash them?

Year 2 – As above but they could estimate how many they think they have in their box first before they count. They could group their objects into 2's, 5's or 10's to count more quickly. Then order the number of objects each pair has found and use ordinal numbers to make a winners' list - from first to last place. They could also find the total the number of objects the whole class has found. (calculator)

Year 3 – Children collect objects in a matchbox and afterwards count and make a winners list. Each pair then makes a tally of the materials their objects are made from – metal / wood / plastic / plant / rock / etc.

Draw a bar chart to show this data.

Year 4 – After they have made a winners list, you could use this opportunity to talk about rounding each sub-total to the nearest 10 - in order to estimate larger totals more accurately, to get a grand total of objects collected.

Add the sub-totals together and see how close the real answer is to the estimate.

All the tallies could be put together and the totals of each material then rounded to the nearest 10. Children can use that data to say what fraction of the total amount each separate material is. For example:

Material	Number	Total	Rounded	Fraction
Wood	卌 卌 卌 卌 卌 IIII	29	30	$^{30}/_{110} = {}^{3}/_{11}$
Metal	卌 卌 卌 卌 卌	25	30	$^{30}/_{110} = {}^{3}/_{11}$
Plastic	卌 卌 III	13	10	$^{10}/_{110} = {}^{1}/_{11}$
Plant	卌 卌 卌 卌 卌 卌 卌 卌 II	42	40	$^{40}/_{110} = {}^{4}/_{11}$

You could also use this opportunity to introduce or revise simplifying fractions.

Year 5 – As above but can they also turn these fractions into percentages?

Year 6 – As above and can they use the percentages to make a pie chart to show the data?

Learning Benefits:

- Gives ownership of the task because they have collected the items themselves
- Healthy competition creates interest in the task
- Miniature scale makes task challenging
- Makes the math of fractions, percentages and statistics real

****

Multiple Choices

Numeracy Focus: *Number – multiplication; division; fractions; percentages; Problem solving.*

Suitable for: KS1 and KS2 – small groups

What you will need:

Use a variety of objects found in your particular environment e.g. cars in the car park / benches / bikes / clover leaves on the field/ daffodils.

What you do:

Make a list of questions similar to those below but appropriate for your class, which will lead them to go out into the environment to find the answer.

Try to make sure the questions are relevant and real-life.

Year 1 - How many headlights in the car park? How many windscreen wipers? How many wing mirrors? How many bike tyres?

Can they draw arrays to help them? (To keep the numbers lower you could ask questions such as: 'How many *silver* wing mirrors altogether?' and 'How many headlights on the *green* cars altogether?)

Discuss the use of 'each' and 'altogether' highlighting the need to make sets or arrays.

Year 2 – As above plus - If half the bike tyres need pumping up, how many would that be?

Pick nine clover leaves – how many smaller lobes altogether?

We want to make bunches of daffodils for Mother's day – if we put 5 flowers in each bunch, how many bunches could we make?

What if we only used 3 flowers for each bunch?

Year 3 – As above plus - How many car tyres are in the car park altogether?

If a quarter of them need pumping up, how many is that?

How many car doors are *red*? (Could be a two-step problem with 2 door and 4 door cars)

Year 4 – The caretaker has said that (*three quarters*) of the *(fence panels)* around the school need re-painting – it will cost £4 for a pot of paint which will cover *(3 panels).*

How much will it cost altogether? How much paint will be left over?

Year 5 – If a quarter of the car tyres in the car park are bald and illegal and they cost £50 each, what would be the total cost to replace them?

What is the fewest number of teachers who might be affected? What is largest number?

Year 6 – If 25% of the car head lights and rear lights in the car park aren't working, how many light bulbs would be needed to replace them?

If rear lights cost £2.50 each and the front ones cost £3.45, what is the total cost?

What is the smallest amount one teacher might have to pay and what is the most they might have to pay?

What is the largest number of cars that might be affected and what is the least?

Learning Benefits:

- Real life scenarios make numeracy relevant
- Use of vocabulary for word problems
- Team work and cooperation
- Supports NC 2014 Programmes of Study for Maths

****

Nature Search

Numeracy Focus: *Addition*

Suitable for: KS1

What you will need:

An outside area rich in natural objects or you may need to enrich it with items such as feathers, twigs, leaves, snail shells, pebbles, pine cones etc.

2 x 3 grid with a picture of a natural object and a point score next to it (laminated for re-use).

(If you are really lacking in natural objects then choose other manmade items to hide such as paperclips, treasury tags etc.)

What you do:

Give pairs of children a 2x3 grid. Differentiate the point scores according to the adding ability of your children.

Give the children a certain amount of time to find the objects and at the end of that time they add up their scores. Who scored the most?

Learning Benefits:

- Active learning
- Healthy competition
- Supports NC 2014 Programmes of Study for Maths

Operation Inverse

Numeracy Focus: *Number facts and families. Four operations. Inverse operations. Roman numerals.*

Suitable for: KS1 and KS2

What you will need:

Clipboards; paper and pens; number cards appropriate for the ability of children and enough for the number of teams you have:

Year 1 – 1-10

Year 2 – 1-20 / tens numbers to 100

Year 3 – 1-12

Year 4 – three digit numbers and a set of single digit numbers

Year 5 – numbers written in Roman numerals

Year 6 – 1-12

What you do:

Hide the appropriate number cards around the outdoor space and split the children into small teams.

Year 1 / 2 - ask them to find 2 numbers and add them together.

Then they need to write down as many number sentences as they can with the three numbers in that number family using + / - / =

They then replace the cards and look for more to make more number fact families.

After a certain amount of time the team with the most number families is the winner.

Year 3 – as above but use x and ÷

Year 4 – ask children to find a three digit and a single digit number; multiply them to find the third number and use x and ÷

Year 5 – find two numbers written in Roman numerals and use + and −

Year 6 – find three numbers, investigate and write down all the possible answers for those three numbers using all four operations and brackets.

For example;

2+1 x 3 = 5
(2+1) x 3 = 9
3+1 x 2 = 5
(3+1) x 2 = 8.......and so on

Learning Benefits:

- Active learning
- Team-work
- Supports NC 2014 Programmes of Study for Maths

****

Pairs

Numeracy Focus: *number facts to 10 and 20*

Suitable for: KS1 and early KS2 consolidation– whole class split into groups.

What you will need: Any large space; enough balls / beanbags (depending on gross motor skills) for each group.

What you do:

Number bonds for all numbers 1-10 / and number bonds for 100 in multiples of ten.

Split the class into groups depending on what total number you want them to know the number bonds for.

Groups make a circle and are numbered from 0 to the total number but make sure you double up on the number double if there is one i.e. if you want them to make 10 you will need 13 children numbered 0, 1, 2, 3, 4, **5, 5,** 6, 7, 8, 9, 10 and a centre child. If you want them to make 7, you will need 8 children numbered 0, 1, 2, 3, 4, 5, 6, 7 and a centre child.

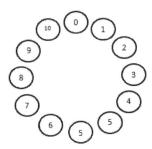

Tell them which number they are working with. The child in the centre throws the ball to number 1 and that child shouts their number. The child who has the number to make the bond shouts out their number and the ball is thrown to them. The ball is then thrown back to the centre child, who then throws it out again to number two. The aim should be to get finished quicker each time.

When they have mastered the pairs in order, the centre child then throws the ball randomly each time, making sure everyone has a turn.

If you have two or three equal circles of children can they beat each other?

Number bonds for 20

For number bonds to 20 number the children 0 to 10. Child number 1 stands in the middle and throws the ball to any child. That child shouts out their own number and this time the others all shout the matching number, whilst the centre child and the one who has the ball change places. Keep repeating and swapping the centre child until they have all had a turn in the middle.

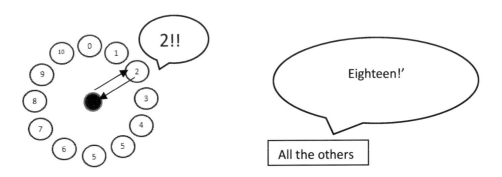

Problem solving / Thinking:

If they wanted to make the number 40 – what could they number themselves? Can they make up a game to practise some number bonds for 50?

Learning Benefits:

- Increases concentration because the ball may be thrown at them!
- Working together to increase their speed
- Actively reinforces number bonds
- Collective thinking doesn't put anyone 'on the spot'
- Supports NC 2014 Programmes of Study for Maths

****

Paperboy

Numeracy Focus: *Number - odds and evens*

Suitable for: KS1 – whole class

What you will need:

Outdoor space; neighbouring street (do a reconnaissance or you may come unstuck with strange numbering); clipboards; paper and pens per pair; a shoulder bag of old magazines and newspapers clearly marked with house numbers that correspond to however many children you have.

What you do:

Go out into a street (in smaller groups, if possible) and look at how the houses are numbered.

Start at number 1 and walk down the street to about number 19, and ask children to write down the numbers of the houses on their clipboard.

Cross the street and ask the children to write the numbers on this side on the other side of their paper.

Back in the playground ask children to look at the numbers they have written. What do they notice?

Re-create the street on the playground by asking children to line up as houses on either side of a 'road'.

How should we number the houses?

Can each side of children shout out their numbers in turn?

Choose a 'paper boy' to deliver the papers in the shoulder bag in consecutive order.

Problem solving / Thinking

Year 1 – What do the children notice? (He has to keep crossing the road.)

How could he make it easier for himself? (Sort out the papers into odds and evens beforehand). Do the sorting and start again.

Can they all tell the paperboy whether the number is odd or even when he shouts it out?

How do they know which are odd and even numbers?

Year 2 - Take the children on the same walk as above.

How much time do they estimate that he saves doing all the odds first then the evens?

How much distance does he save?

How could they work it out?

Learning Benefits

- Real-life scenario
- Actively maths with a purpose
- Supports NC 2014 Programmes of Study for Maths

****

Photo Shoot

Numeracy Focus: *Number – multiplication. Problem solving*

Suitable for: Lower KS2

What you will need:

A large play space; dressing up clothes for 4 teams – for each team 2-6 of one kind of item and 2-6 of another but vary the amount you give to each team.

For example; 3 hats and 4 shirts / 4 scarves and 3 shirts / 2 hats and 6 T- shirts / 6 skirts and 2 scarves.

 4 digital cameras.

What you do:

Split the class into 4 teams and give each a set of clothes and a camera.

The task is to photograph everyone in the team (at least once) in as many different combinations of clothes that they can.

No-one must wear the same as anyone else - get them to check the photos they have already taken to make sure.

Back in class, download the photographs and count how many combinations they have. (They should all have 12 so get them to try to find the combinations they don't have if they are short.)

As a class think about the numbers involved in each team's photo shoot - for example; 3 hats and 4 shirts = 12 different outfits.

Do they notice any relationship between the numbers?

Try it out again with smaller/larger numbers of clothes – does the formula still work?

Learning Benefits:

- Active and fun
- Real – life objects and scenario
- Investigation
- Team-work
- Supports NC 2014 Programmes of Study for Maths
- Cross-curricular links - ICT

****

Pi

Numeracy Focus: *Algebra. Problem solving.*

Suitable for: Year 6 in groups - follow on from the activity *Squash!*

What you will need:

Chalk; small garden cane; string ; calculators - enough for each group.

What you do:

Ask each group to make a set of large compasses from chalk, a small garden cane and string.

Would a circle fit more people in than a square?

How could we test it fairly?

Check they know the equation for calculating areas of different basic shapes.

How do we work out the area of a circle? ($A = \pi r^2$)

If your calculators don't have pi on them use 3.14.

Example:

Area = pi x radius² $\longrightarrow$ radius of the circle is 6cm $\longrightarrow$ 3.14 x 6²

$\longrightarrow$ 3.14 x 36

$\longrightarrow$ 113.04cm²

What is the smallest circle that six people could fit into?

Try it out. What are the radius and the area?

Can they estimate what the radius would be for the smallest circle that would fit the whole class in?

Can they think of any other real life uses for knowing the area of a circle? (E.g garden design / architecture.)

If you know the area of a circle, how do you find the area of a semi-circle? Or a quarter circle?

Learning Benefits:

- Fun activity that shows algebra has a practical use
- Team-work involves everyone
- Supports NC 2014 Programmes of Study for Maths

****

Play Dough

Numeracy Focus: *Measurement – mass, volume, non-standard units.*

Suitable for: KS1

What you will need:

Water tray; sand tray or table in an outside area; recipe cards or a large poster; large bowl; plastic cup; teaspoon; tablespoon; fork; aprons; plastic or latex gloves (optional – if they use a fork they shouldn't get neat food colour on their hands).

Year 2 – the above + weighing scales

What you do:

Year 1 - Let the children make their own play-dough from the recipe in pairs – each batch makes enough for two to play with, is very supple and it will last a long time if you keep it in a plastic bag.

1 cup plain flour
½ cup salt
1 cup water (boiling, from the kettle)
1 teaspoon of food colouring
2 tablespoons cream of tartar
1 tablespoons cooking oil
glitter (optional!)

Mix all the dry ingredients together.

Make a well in the middle and put all the wet ingredients in.

Get an adult to support adding the boiling water.

Use the fork to mix it all together hot.

When all are combined, leave to cool for a couple of minutes and knead on the table with hands.

You can use the following recipe if you want a recipe with cold water that children can do by themselves, but the texture isn't as good and it isn't as pliable - so it depends how long you want the finished dough to last.

3 cups of plain flour
2 tablespoons of corn flour
1 cup of salt
1 cup of cold water
2 teaspoons of vegetable oil
2 teaspoons of food colouring or paint

Mix all the dry ingredients together.

Make a well in the middle and put all the wet ingredients in.

Mix until combined and then knead on the table.

Year 2 – As above but they could convert the recipe to grams by measuring the mass of a 'cup' of each ingredient using weighing scales before they make it.

Learning Benefits:

- Active, messy fun
- Real-life
- Supports NC 2014 Programmes of Study for Maths
- Cross curricular links – Science. DT. Art

****

Playing Card PE

Numeracy Focus: *Counting. Mental addition, multiplication and division.*

Suitable for: KS1 and lower KS2

What you will need: Large outdoor space; pack of large playing cards (with the digits covered for Year 1); posters with heart, diamond, club, spade and the name or picture of an exercise on e.g. star jumps / spotty dogs / toe touches / sprinting between two cones.

What you do:

Put a poster in different corners or areas of your space and tell the children what exercise they have to do in each area.

Place the playing cards in the middle.

Year 1 - The children each pick a card from the central pile.

They go to the corresponding area with the card, count the icons and perform the relevant number of exercises. For example; if the card has 8 hearts then they do 8 star jumps.

When they have finished they return the card to the middle and choose another.

Year 1 and 2 – have each child choose two cards and add them together to give them the total repetitions they need to do.

Year 2 - organise children in teams and use cards from Ace to 5 in the central pile(s).

One child from each team chooses two cards from the pile and takes them to their team.

They multiply them together and then share out the task so that the total number is completed.

It doesn't have to be equal at Year 2. For example if they choose the 10 and 2 of spades but there are 6 of them in the team they can share it so that they all do some each as long as the total is completed.

Year 3 / 4 – as above but have the whole pack and divide equally and have one child perform the remainder afterwards.

Learning Benefits:

- Active learning
- Supports NC 2014 Programmes of Study for Maths
- Cross-curricular links - PE

Pop!

Numeracy Focus: *Measurement – volume and capacity. Problem solving.*

Suitable for: KS2 - in teams.

What you will need:

Water bomb balloons; water trays or builders' trays and buckets; access to lots of water; measuring jugs; paper and pens; enough buckets for one per team. (you might want to have a bag on standby for wet PE kit)

What you do:

Thinking questions:

What is the largest amount of water that can be put in a balloon before it bursts?

This will need children think about their best way to measure and record the amounts they put in.

How do they make sure the test is fair?

Next is a timed team challenge: Move as much water as you can, into a bucket at the end of the course, but using only 6 water balloons between you.

You can make this harder by getting them to run with the balloon between their knees or give them some obstacles to climb over or under whilst carrying it!

Do they fill up the balloon as much as they can and take the risk of it bursting or do they play it safe?

What is the optimum fill level for the task??

Measure the water in the buckets at the end to see who has won.

Ask children to design a different volume /capacity challenge using another material – such as sand – and different containers.

Set a more open-ended challenge – i.e. here are some containers / bags to choose from.

You can choose just 3 different ones to move all that sand / soil / coloured liquid to that large pond/ sand pit.

What is the most efficient way to do that?

Part way through the task they have to give back one of the original containers they chose – which one will they choose to return? Why?

Learning Benefits:

- Active, messy and fun
- Investigating
- Maths with a purpose
- Team-work
- Supports NC 2014 Programmes of Study for Maths
- Cross-curricular link - Science

Pots and Pans

Numeracy Focus: *Measurement – volume and capacity. Number – multiplication. Problem solving.*

Suitable for: KS2 – years 4 /5 in pairs

What you will need:

Water tray; pots and pans of various sizes; an old kettle with the cord and plug cut off; if possible a school tea urn; measuring jugs; cups.

What you do:

Estimate how much each pot or pan holds and then investigate using measuring jugs.

Record the capacity of each one and give the result in millilitres and then convert to litres.

Some possible thinking questions: (decide which are most appropriate for each group):

How many small pans does it take to fill the biggest pan?

How many cups of tea could we make from the kettle? Try out some different sized cups and mugs.

If you have an urn – or large teapot - how many cups of tea could you make from one full urn (or the largest teapot you have)?

We need to provide at least 200 cups of tea at the school fair. How many times will we have to fill the urn and/or the teapot?

How many cups from one teapot? Is there a big difference in the number of cups we get out of the teapot if we use smaller / larger cups?

If the cost of one litre of water is (insert a figure commensurate with their ability), how much will it cost for the water for the school fair?

Add in the cost of tea, sugar and milk – what should be charged for a cup of tea?

How much profit are we likely to make?

Learning Benefits:

- Active learning
- Real – life objects and scenario
- Investigation
- Team-work
- Supports NC 2014 Programmes of Study for Maths

Shape Hunt

Numeracy Focus: *Geometry - shape properties*

Suitable for: KS1 and KS2 – small groups

What you will need:

Shape property cards; 2D drawings of 3D shapes; nets of 3D shapes or pictures of nets cards; 2D or 3D shapes in a bag.

What you do:

Hide the shape cards in the area where you are working.

Children choose a shape in turn from the bag and taking the shape with them look for the correct card that matches their shape.

They must leave the incorrect cards where they are and continue looking for the right one.

When they have all finished, ask the group to share their answers and see if they are correct.

The children put their card back in the bag and go to hide their shape.

They then take a property card from the bag. Everyone goes to find their correct shape to match to a card.

You could also do this as a competition in teams to get back first with the right answer.

Year 1 - circle / square / triangle / rectangle / hexagon / pentagon

Year 2 - circle / square / triangle / rectangle / hexagon / pentagon / octagon

Year 3 - diamond / kite / cube / cuboid / pyramid / sphere / cylinder

Year 4 - right-angle triangle / isosceles triangle / scalene triangle / equilateral triangle / parallelogram / trapezium / rhombus

Year 5 - 2D representations of 3D shapes

Year 6 - nets of 3D shapes

There could be bonus points for finding shapes in the outdoor space that match the card(s)

E.g. a triangle that forms part of the bench legs

A circle (maybe not a perfect one) – seen as a knot on a tree trunk.

Children describe the shapes they see in the environment but also be able to describe why it often only 'close' to being the 'perfect' shape: they practise using the correct mathematical language.

e.g. 'This corner of the field is almost a right angle – but not quite 90 degrees because of the mud'

'The canes being used in the garden for the beans almost form a pyramid but they don't quite come to a sharp point at the top because of the string.'

Learning Benefits:

- Active maths
- Recognising shapes outside the classroom and in the natural environment
- Supports NC 2014 Programmes of Study for Maths

Slalom Run

Numeracy Focus: *Number – multiplication; division / tables*

Suitable for: KS1 and KS2 – Whole class

What you will need:

4 sets of cards with answers for the times table you want to practise (these could be one or a mixture); 4 sets of PE cones – enough to span the course you design; handheld whiteboard and pen.

What you do:

Set out the cones, in four lines, as a slalom run for each team.

Place one set of answer cards at the end of each line.

Write a question on the whiteboard; everyone calls out the question but they only discuss the answer with their team.

Team members then take it in turns to run the slalom and find the answer in the set of cards.

The first child to bring the correct answer back gets a point for their team.

Taking it further:

Make sets of cards with the questions on.

Write the answer on the whiteboard and get them to find the correct question at the end of the slalom.

The same game can be played using division tables.

If you want to incorporate it with PE skills use hockey sticks and balls or footballs to make the slalom more difficult.

Learning Benefits:

- Active learning
- Teamwork
- By everyone calling out the question, the children learn the times table in a fun way and in a random order.
- Supports NC 2014 Programmes of Study for Maths
- Cross-curricular links – PE

Sort it Out!

Numeracy Focus: *Statistics - Carroll diagrams*

Suitable for: Lower KS2 – whole class

What you will need:

PE mats x 4 - or chalk; large criteria labels; cards with odd and even numbers in single and double digits – enough for the class.

What you do:

Put four PE mats on the playground as a Carroll diagram or mark out a Carroll diagram on the playground.

Label the mats with the information you want to sort.

Example:

	girl	boy
Pet		
no pet		

Children place themselves on the mat in the correct place. You can then change the criteria labels to girl / boy / brothers and sisters / no brothers or sisters and get them into pairs.

They question their partner and place them in the right place on the mats.

Do a random check by questioning the children on the mat as to whether the information is true.

Now change the criteria to odd / even / single digit / double digit.

Children have a card each but work in pairs to decide where to put their cards.

Can children think of other criteria where a Carroll diagram might be useful?

Are there some things that are more difficult to categorise in this way? E.g. large pet / small pet or (would we need more clarification?)

Can statistics always be relied upon to give a clear black and white picture?

Learning Benefits:

- Active maths
- Whole body experience
- Paired work – cooperation
- Supports NC 2014 Programmes of Study for Maths

Spell Check

Numeracy Focus: *Number - read and write numbers in words.*

Suitable for: KS1 and KS2 in pairs

What you will need:

Year 1 and 2 - Type up the words they need to spell and make two copies on card.

Leave one copy as the full word and cut up the other to make letter cards – these can be individual letters or graphemes e.g. e <u>igh</u> t: f <u>i</u> v <u>e</u>: <u>t w</u> o: f <u>ou</u> r t <u>ee</u> n.

If you leave some room under the full word and laminate it, the children can copy the word underneath using white board pens and cloths.

Year 3 and 4 – Number cards written in figures on one side and words on the other.

What you do:

Hide the letters in the environment and give each pair a word card. They then go and find the letters, match up and then look, cover, write, check it.

Year 1 – one two three four five six seven eight nine ten eleven twelve thirteen fourteen fifteen sixteen seventeen eighteen nineteen twenty.

Year 2 – thirty forty fifty sixty seventy eighty ninety hundred.

Hide the number cards in figures in the environment.

Child A finds a number, takes it to B and reads it out loud.

B then writes it on the white board in words.

A checks the spelling on the back of the card.

Year 3/4 – random numbers to one thousand.

Can children think of different strategies for learning the spellings?

Shapes of words, words within words, making the shapes of the letters with their bodies, mnemonics for some of them.

Give children an opportunity to share their own successful strategies with each other.

Taking it further:

You can also do this for the spelling of other mathematical words which are appropriate for their ability.

See *Shape Hunt* for the age appropriate words they need to know for geometry.

Learning Benefits:

- Active learning
- Paired learning and cooperation
- Cross-curricular links - English

Sports Weigh In

Numeracy Focus: *Measurement – mass. Problem solving*

Suitable for: Upper KS2

What you will need: 4- 5 sets of bathroom scales; calculators; 4-5 rucksacks; variety of weights 500g-1kg (several for each team).

What you do:

Explain what a weigh-in is for at a sporting event, for example horse racing, weight lifting and boxing (so that no-one has an unfair advantage).

You could show photos of a heavyweight boxer and a flyweight boxer. Would it be fair to let them compete against each other or would one have an advantage?

Jockeys also have to 'weigh out' at the start of the race and if they are too light they have to wear extra weights for the race and repeat it at the end of the race.

The challenge is to put the class into 'fair' teams for a sports competition that involves moving heavy objects.

(If you do have children who weigh vastly outside of the norm of your class then you will have to be really sensitive about how you do this. You may decide not to do it at all.)

You will need to discuss how taller people are likely to weigh more but that we are all different. Some children have a bigger skeleton than others – the children shouldn't compare themselves to others of their age but think about whether they are a healthy weight based on their height.

There are likely to be weights ranging from;

27 kg (60lbs / 4st 3) to 50kg (90lbs / 6st 4).

In groups of about six, children need to weigh themselves and record their weights on a card both in metric and imperial measures – if imperial measures are used in sport it is often in pounds rather than stones and pounds.

They then have to order themselves as a whole class in a line from the lightest to the heaviest. Then split the line into 4-5 weight bands. These become the teams for the competition.

Tell the children that one game will be to carry weights in a rucksack on an obstacle course - do they think the lightest people should carry more so that they weigh the same as the others or should the heavier people carry more weight because they are bigger and possibly stronger? How much more weight?

Let them try out the different weights. Let each team decide what they think the rules should be.

Come back together and discuss it. Agree the rules and try it out. Was it fair?

Can the teams think of another game where weight or height might be an advantage or disadvantage and make a rule which makes it fair?

Learning Benefits:

- Active learning
- Real – life scenario
- Investigation
- Team-work
- Supports NC 2014 Programmes of Study for Maths
- Cross-curricular links - PHSE

Squash

Numeracy Focus: *Problem solving. Measure – length, perimeter and area. Geometry – shape.*

Suitable for: KS1 and KS2

What you will need:

Outdoor space; pictures that depict people taking up the challenge of fitting as many people as possible into a telephone box or small car (use a search engine); tape measures; calculators; pens and paper for years 5 and 6.

What you do:

Introduce the activity with a picture depicting a lot of people trying to fit into the smallest space possible.

Explain that it wouldn't be safe to try and stand on top of each other and that each person has to have at least one foot on the ground.

If they haven't done this activity before then you may need to work them through from the Year 1 activity, using your judgement as you go.

Year 1 – Have several 1m squares marked up in chalk on the playground.

Use one with the whole class. How many children do they think would fit into it? What if we divided the square into two?

Do half the original number fit into it?

What if the halves were triangles?

Let them test it out.

Have other sized squares marked up and let them test them out in the same way?

Does it help if the people are ordered in lines or is 'squashing' better?

Year 2 - Groups of 6. What is the smallest square that 6 children can fit into?

Can they measure the length of its sides?

What is the best shape for 6 people to fit into?

Try some out.

Year 3/4 - Challenge in groups.

What is the size of the smallest square that the whole class could fit into?

Test it out by sampling their group.

What is the length of the sides of the square that would be needed?

What is the perimeter of the square?

Year 5/6 – How many children can fit into the 1m square?

Talk about doubling its area? Is that still a square?

What about the perimeter?

What would the length of the sides be of a square that had an area of $2m^2$?

What area would a square with sides of 2m length have?

Let them have pens and paper to draw their jottings.

Learning Benefits:

- estimating
- working as a group
- builds on previous learning
- applying what they find out - investigating
- supports NC 2014 Programmes of Study for Maths

****

Targets

Numeracy Focus: *Addition. Subtraction*

Suitable for: KS1 and KS2

What you will need: Target boards chalked on the playground for each group; beanbags.

What you do:

Game 1 - Decide on a score for each area of the target depending on the ability of the class or each group – for upper KS2 you could use fractions or decimals.

Each child in the group throws 3 beanbags onto the target and they add up the scores. Highest score wins.

Game 2 – All groups have the same numbers on their target board and compete against each other. They have to see which group can make the target number you give them using the fewest number of beanbags.

Game 3 – They could practise subtraction by being given a starting number and racing down to zero using as few beanbags as possible.

Learning Benefits:

- Active learning
- Cross-curricular links - PE
- Supports NC 2014 Programmes of Study for Maths

****

Time and duration

<u>Numeracy Focus:</u> *Telling analogue time and time durations. Practical demonstration.*

<u>Suitable for:</u> KS1 and KS2

<u>What you will need:</u> Large clock chalked on the playground; one short and one longer skipping rope for the clock hands.

<u>What you do:</u>

Year 1/2/3/4 - Telling the time – Arrange 12 children around the clock on the numbers.

Stand in the middle holding one end of both skipping ropes.

Ask one child to take the end of the short rope and one to take the end of the long rope.

Get them to act as the 'hands' and stand in the 12 o'clock position.

Call out a time appropriate for the ability of your class. Ask the children who think they are standing where the hands should be to raise their hand, so that children holding the 'hands' can move to the correct place.

Any children who are not part of the clock can adjudicate.

For older children, mark in the minutes on the clock and use times to the nearest minute.

Year 3 / 4 - Durations – set the children out as above but give them a real-life scenario with a starting time and a finishing time appropriate to the ability of your children.

For *Year 4* – use scenarios where they convert between minutes and hours.

The 'hand' children place themselves on the start time and then move round.

As they are doing so the other children count in 5's as the minute hand moves to each number around the clock.

For example:

- Doctor Who starts at 7 o'clock and finishes an hour later? What do they notice about where the minute hand ends up?

- Dad starts washing the car at half past two and finishes at twenty three minutes past three. How long did he take?

Learning Benefits:

- Active learning
- Team-work
- Supports NC 2014 Programmes of Study for Maths

****

Turning Point

Numeracy Focus: *Geometry - shape and angles.*

Suitable for: KS2 in groups of three

What you will need: 2 skipping ropes per group.

What you do:

One child takes one end of both skipping ropes (Child A) and the other two pick up the other two spare ends (Child B and Child C).

Year 3/4 – Ask children to create a **right angle** and then angles which are bigger than (**obtuse**) and smaller than a right angle (**acute**).

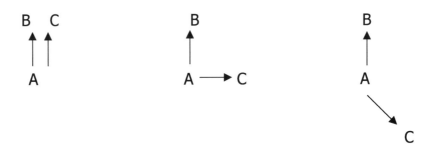

A and B stand still whilst C turns a series of right angles – how many right angles have they turned altogether?

What do we call this in terms of turns?

How many right angles make a three quarter turn?

How many a complete turn?

Year 5/6 - Children could be asked to make **reflex** angles (angles bigger than 180°).

Child A and Child B stand still as the third child marks the right angles that they could make, moving around Child A as the pivot point.

How many degrees would 2 right angles make? And 3? And 4?

Most of them will have heard the terms 'pulling a 360' or 'a 180' on their bikes or skateboards.

What does that mean?

Get someone to demonstrate the amount of turn.

Use the mouth of a goal to set out a series of different angles with the ropes.

Which angles are good for goal scoring? Why?

Learning Benefits:

- Active maths
- Real-life scenario
- Supports NC 2014 Programmes of Study for Maths

****

Twins

Numeracy Focus: *Number doubles and halving.*

Suitable for: KS1 and KS2 – Grouping depends on the size of number doubles that you want to practise. In KS2 when the children can do larger number doubles then you could use the whole class in one circle.

What you will need: Outdoor space.

What you do:

Each group makes a circle. Number the children round, as in this example, 1-5 for doubles to 10.

Make sure they have a reasonable distance to run in and aren't too squashed.

Example: for a group of 10 number round from 1-5 and then 1-5 again.

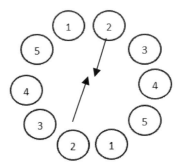

Explain that the children are going to join with their 'twin number' to make it double.

Encourage them to think about what their number double would be.

You then shout out the number that you want to make, in this case '4', and the two children that make that number run into the middle.

When they get to the middle they shout their numbers (one is likely to get there quicker) one shouts '2' and then the other shouts '2' and then the whole group shouts 'Double 2 is 4 – half of 4 is 2' .

The 'twins' then go back into the circle.

Continue until they have all had a turn. Re-number the circle so they all get a different number and start again.

Taking it further:

With more able children start from a higher number when numbering the circle to allow for higher number doubles.

To add a visual dimension you could produce large number cards for each child to hold up when they get to the middle.

Learning Benefits:

- Children have to think what double their number is and whether their number is half of the number required.
- Joining with someone else consolidates the sense of 'double-ness'.
- Twinning with a different person each time ensures they 're-think' and don't just join with the same person
- If they are unsure, their twin may have shouted out the number already so that they can run in when they hear it.

****

Venn Diagrams

Numeracy Focus: *Statistics - Venn diagrams. Number – multiplication tables.*

Suitable for: Upper KS1 and KS2 – whole class and groups of three.

What you will need: Any large outdoor space; chalk; number cards; blank cards.

What you do:

Draw two large overlapping circles in chalk.

Year 2 - use criteria such as 'have a brother / have a sister' and ask children to position themselves in the correct circle.

What if you have both?

Who will stand in the intersection?

What about those without any siblings?

Repeat with 'have a cat / have a dog' etc.

Give two hoops per group and ask them to lay them out as a Venn diagram.

Year3/4/5 – Have, for example, 'in the 2 times table' and 'in the 6 times table' as the criteria.

Give them all a number card (including some not in either table) and ask them to place the card in the correct place.

Can children think of their own number criteria?

In groups of three, use three hoops and make their own number cards to fit the criteria or give them a set of cards and ask them to work out the criteria.

Year 6 – Continue to practise multiples as a class but also try factors of other numbers; e.g. '48' and '60'.

Use the opportunity to revise knowledge of terminology – universal set / intersection. Introduce the term union.

Game: Draw a universal set on the playground, for example ' numbers 1-100' with subsets of (multiples of 12) and b (multiples of 4) overlapping in the middle.

Give each child a number card and get them to arrange themselves in the set as per the criteria.

When they are arranged get the various parts of the universal set to perform an action or sit down.

You might give the commands:

➢ Universal set - sit down.
➢ A union - B hop.
➢ A intersect - B hands in the air
➢ A complement sit down (everything in the universal set except A)
➢ B complement star jumps (everything in the universal set except B)

They could all swap numbers, re-position themselves and play again.

Learning Benefits:

- Active maths
- Team-work
- Supports NC 2014 Programmes of Study for Maths

****

We're all going on a.....Bus Trip

Numeracy Focus: *Measurement - money and time. Number - giving change.*

Suitable for: KS2 – whole class or small group.

What you will need: Adults to provide the ratio to children to accompany the trip; local bus timetables; local OS maps; envelopes; prepared maths trail; clipboards (optional)

What you do:

Year 3/4 – Plan a round trip bus journey from the bus stop nearest to the school to a distance you have sufficient time to get to.

If it is a simple bus journey with no long stop over at a destination point you could provide a maths trail to be done on the bus (*see the Maths Trails for your Year group at the back of the book for some ideas*).

(Obviously, you will need to do a reconnaissance mission for the journey, to be able to plan it beforehand.)

To prepare for the trip the children work out the coins they might use to pay for it.

You can give the children some different scenarios with amounts and change from a variety of coins or notes up to £50.

They can look at the timetable to see what time the buses are and some can work out how long the journey will take.

What time is there a return bus? Where do they catch it?

They then choose coins to go in their own envelope so that they have the right money to pay with on the day (Bus drivers do not like having to give change – especially for 25 children!)

Year 5 / 6 – In groups plan a real trip on the bus for themselves from the nearest bus stop to the school to a destination point.

You will need to give them maps to see what landmarks or parks etc. are on or near to the route.

The class vote for the best trip.

The children have to work out how much their trip will cost, use timetables to see if they need to change buses and how long the journey will take, use maps to follow the route and work out the distance of the round trip.

They could plan what to do at the destination point if it is something of interest and then write a persuasive letter home proposing the trip and asking for the funds from their parents.

If you just want to get them to plan a round trip journey, rather than stop off anywhere, you could set a maths trail for the route.

Learning Benefits:

- Real life activity – Maths with a purpose
- Healthy competition in teams
- Cross-curricular links – Geography (local area / maps and plans). English

****

What's the time Mr Wolf?

Numeracy Focus: *Measurement – time.*

Suitable for: KS1 and KS2 – 2 or 3 groups of about 10 - mixed ability.

What you will need:

Large clocks (2m diameter) chalked out on playground with a centre point marked on.

What you do:

Split each group of about 10 children into 2 groups.

One group is going to be the 'hour hand team' and should have about 4 children in it and the other group will be the 'minute hand team' and have about 6 children in it.

The children call out 'What's the time, Mr / Mrs / Miss (insert adults name)? The teacher calls out a time.

Year 1 - o'clock / half past

Year 2 – half past / quarter past / quarter to / to 5 minutes.

Year 3/ 4 / 5/ 6 - all other times. (From Year 3 you could also use Roman numerals)

The children then align themselves to move their 'hand' to the right place on the clock. When they are sure they are positioned correctly they sit down in place. First team correctly positioned get the points.

Make sure that when you ask them to make times other than o'clock that the 'hour hand team' in each group position themselves correctly and are not pointed directly at the hour number (make this a teaching point).

Taking it further:

Demonstrate the drawing of the clock to the children and teach them to write on the 12, then the 6, then the 3 and the 9, and to fill in the other numbers after.

Then you could ask the children to write the numbers on their clock themselves so that there is less preparation when you want to play this again.

You could introduce a seconds hand. Ask the children to walk around the clock in what they think is 60 seconds. Check their estimations with a stop watch.

How many skips can you do in 20 seconds? How many in 45?

How many seconds does it take for all your team members to hop to the bench and back?

Estimate and test each other.

Learning Benefits:

- Whole body experience aids memory as all the children have to position themselves correctly.
- They need to work as a team if they want to win.
- Anyone who is of a lower ability or is unsure can follow the others until they feel confident themselves.
- Supports NC 2014 Programmes of Study for Maths

****

Wheels on the Bus

Numeracy Focus: *Measurement – money. Number – counting, addition, subtraction (giving change).*

Suitable for: KS1 – whole class in small groups (can be mixed ability or grouped according to want to achieve)

What you will need:

Large play space; 5-6 cones and poles to use as 'bus stops' and marked with names of activity zones; cash boxes; money – real or play; slips of paper with names of bus stops (colours) - enough for each child; money belt for the driver; numeracy, PE or cross curricular activities set up at the bus stops; laminated 'tickets' in colours of the bus stops; one bus driver (although having two can sometimes save long queues).

What you do:

Set out bus stops around the playground or field. Employ a bus driver (teacher or another adult to begin with).

Give each group a slip of paper to tell them which zone they are going to on the bus and money in the denominations appropriate for the level they are working at.

Each group goes to the same destination together as a team, so they can discuss which coins they need / how much change they need; no-one must be left behind.

At the 'Bus station' put a poster stating the cost to go to the certain coloured activity zones, so that the children have to work out from a table how much money they need. They then pay from their group's bank of money and 'buy' a coloured ticket each.

At the zones there are activities set up – you could differentiate the stops in any curriculum subject with independent activities, so that you target key skills for certain groups of children.

Alternatively, you could set up a round robin of independent activities or PE activities at each stop and when the children have finished they get a different slip (from an adult – the bus driver has collected the slips previously), check the poster to see how much they need for that stop, take the correct money from their group's bank and get back on the 'bus'.

Year 1 – Use pennies to pay for 1:1 correspondence. More able children could be given other denominations.

Year 2 – The children decide on which combinations of coins they could have to pay for their own ticket and take the coins from their bank. If you want to focus on giving change, then plan for the denominations to be too big so that they have to check if they have the correct change from the bus driver.

Problem solving - you could make sure there is only enough money to pay for all of the group so that they can't all choose the same denominations as each other to pay with. When they find they don't have enough of the coins they wanted to use they will have to have a rethink and find different ways to pay for everyone with the coins they do have.

This will then give them an insight when they are asked questions such as 'What is the least amount of coins you could pay with? What is the most?'

Learning Benefits:

- Real life scenario
- Working as a team means everyone can succeed
- Can be used at various times throughout the year to build on the learning
- Supports NC 2014 Programmes of Study for Maths
- The activity zones can be made cross-curricular
- An activity that can repeated many times

Maths Outdoor Trails

The following pages provide examples of maths trail questions and activities.

Maths trails not only help children improve their maths skills but also provide opportunities to be more observant, collaborative, independent and thoughtful about their immediate environment.

Learning outdoors should be a fundamental part of every child's experience and there is a great deal of evidence to demonstrate the positive impact of learning outside the classroom.

The first six pages in this section of the book provide 20 generic ideas covering a range of mathematical concepts – of varying levels of difficulty.

The second section has a page per year group - more specifically targeted in terms of ability and linked to the new curriculum. However, these can also be easily adapted for your children.

On the Thinking Child website – in the Free Downloads Section – you will be able to access these pages in Word format, so you can change and adapt them to suit your own outdoor space(s) and children's stage of development.

If you have ideas for maths trails to share with other schools, please feel free to send them into us at info@thinkingchild.org.uk

We will add them to the free download section on the site: www.thinkingchild.org.uk – with full acknowledgements of course.

Maths Outdoors

1.   Look around you. What can you see that has a mathematical connection?

Write or draw any mathematical words or shapes in and around the space you are in.

_____   _____   _____   _____

Write down in words or draw a mathematical sum.

2.   With your group can you make some outdoor 'maths art'?

Each person in your group thinks of a different shape (straight line, star, triangle)

Then line up in different ways to form a human sculpture.

What natural materials or other objects are there in your space to make a piece of art from?

Can you make a frame with sticks?

Or a repeating pattern?

3.   Have a look around and choose 3 or 4 buildings or objects (like a bench).

Can you stand in a space that is the same distance from all the things you have chosen. Estimate the distance.

Now test your estimate by pacing between each one. How close were you? Did you get it right? - yes/no/nearly/miles out? Re-calculate your central position and try again. (Remember that the smaller the object the closer you need to be to it).

Maths Outdoors

4. Go to a wall or pavement/path nearby. What patterns can you see?

Draw a section of it and then continue to repeat the pattern.

What shape(s) are used?   Do they tessellate?

5. Look around and think about what might be the riskiest parts of the area? What sort of things could happen there and why? What is the probability of an accident?

6. On the outside doors of the school – do they all turn clockwise or anti-clockwise – or is there a mixture? What proportion of the handles turn clockwise?

7. Are the doors at the front of the school symmetrical?   How do you know?
Can you draw/measure them?

8. What shape is the letter box? Can you see other shapes like this? Where are they?

9. Face the school. Look at the bricks. What angle is the corner of the bricks? What angle is the corner of the school? Are there other angles on the front of the school? (are there sloping window sills for example?)

Can you estimate the number of bricks on one wall? Write down your method for estimating.

10. Go and find a sign on the school or a shelter. Which are the longest words – find the three longest and write them down. Which are the shortest? Count all the letters on the sign. Work out how many times each letter is used. Which letter is used most frequently?

Maths Outdoors

11. Look at the markings on the playground. Ask ten people which of the markings they like to play on the most and make a table/ tally chart of your findings:

Marking	Number of children
Hopscotch	
Ladder	
Shapes	

Which is the favourite playground marking?

Which is the least favourite?

Think of a new marking or pattern you would like to see on the playground. Where is the best place to put it?

How will you know if there is enough space for it?

12. Look at the fences. How many vertical and horizontal bars are used in one part of the fence? Draw this one piece of the fence.

How many vertical bars does it take to make 7 pieces of fencing?

How many other things can you see that have vertical and horizontal lines?

Can you see oblique lines anywhere?

Maths Outdoors

13. Look at the bird table. Draw all the shapes you can see.

Which shape is used the most?

Why might that be?

Draw the shapes you can see in the bird table from two different sides.

Can you draw it from above – a 'birds' eye' view?

How many different angles can you see?

14. Find a bench. How many legs has it got?

How many slats have been used to make it?

How many legs and slats would there be on 6 benches?

If there were 44 legs how many benches would there be?

If the bench is 2 metres long and the wood for the slats costs £2.00 per metre how much does it cost to make all the slats for the bench?

How much for 6 benches?

Maths Outdoors

15. Find a tree and look at one of its leaves closely. How big is the leaf? Is it bigger or smaller than your hand?

How many leaves does it take to cover both of your hands?

What do you think the area of one leaf is?

Fold the leaf in half. Is the leaf symmetrical?   Can you see any more symmetrical shapes nearby?

16. Plan a route around the school for someone else to follow. But you can only use each path once.

Think of at least 5 'landmarks' you want them to notice – do they look left, right up or down to see them?

Alternatively you would draw a 'treasure map' – plot the coordinates or directions so people can find the next clue and eventually find the 'treasure'

17. Use sticks to make a small square frame on the grass. Can you estimate how many blades of grass there might be? Can you find a way to check your answer?

How many different types of grass or plants are there? How many might there be in a metre square? Or a ten metre square?

Maths Outdoors

18. Choose two places to walk between – for example a tree and the edge of the playground. Estimate how long it will take you to walk between two places. Time each other to see who is the nearest.

How many seconds will it take to run or hop or stride?

19. Walk to the sundial. How many sides does it have? How many hours or minutes are marked on it?

What time is it on the sundial?   What time is it on someone's watch? Is the sundial correct? If not – how much difference is there?   If you finish this maths trail in 30 minutes, what time will it be?

20. Use a compass – or let an adult tell you how to find North. Draw and label the four main points of the compass.

What direction is opposite West? What direction is opposite South-East?

Turn to face the East – what can you see? Make a half turn to your right – where are you facing now? Turn 3 right angles anti-clockwise – where are you facing now?

Around the School Maths Trail Year 1

Numeracy Focus: *Number. Shape. Measurement. Problem solving*

Suitable for: KS1 working in pairs

What you will need: Clipboards, trail sheets and pencils

What you do:

Use the template to add in the numbers, situations and locations relevant to your particular school.

You may choose to put the trail in a different order for different pairs/ groups of children.

Learning benefits:

- Children work independently in pairs (unless they need help with the reading)
- They are active
- Shows maths is everywhere
- Supports NC 2014 Programmes of Study for Maths

Year 1 Maths Trail
Start at the main entrance gate

Names...

If you face the school entrance what is on your *left /right*?		How many seats or benches are there?	
How many footsteps does it take from the school gate to the entrance?		How many *tiles* are there on half of the *shelter roof*?	
What shape is the school sign?		How many foot lengths is a bench?	
Draw the pattern of the paving stones *on the path to the office?*		How many windows look out on the playground?	
How many cars on the car park?		What shape is the *??*	
What is one more than the number of cars in the car park?		How many gates are there?	
What is the number of *(red)* cars add the number of *(silver)* cars?		How many steps are there around the school?	
What is the biggest number you can see?		How many hands high is the *climbing frame?*	
What is the smallest number you can see?		How many trees are there?	
How many doors are there on the outside of the building?		Can you find a *(3D shape)*?	

Around the School Maths Trail Year 2

Numeracy Focus: *Number. Geometry. Measurement. Problem solving*

Suitable for: Year 2 working in pairs

What you will need:

Clipboards, trail sheets and pencils

What you do:

Use the template to add in the numbers, situations and locations relevant to your particular school.

You may choose to put the trail in a different order for different pairs/ groups of children.

Learning benefits:

- Children work independently in pairs (some may need help with the reading)
- Active learning
- Shows that Maths is everywhere
- Supports NC 2014 Programmes of Study for Maths

Year 2 Maths Trail
Start at the main entrance gate

Names...

If you face the school entrance what is a quarter turn on your *left /right?*		How many shelters are there?	
What shapes can you see *in the trellis by the front door?*		If 10 children can play in one shelter, how many children can play in the shelters altogether?	
What is the unit number in the telephone number on the school sign?		Estimate how many metres and centimetres the bench is.	
How many paving slabs are there *on the path to the office?*		How many windows that look out on the playground are square?	
How many cars on the car park have a number 6?		Can you find a *3D shape?* What is it and what is the shape called?	
What is ten more than the number of cars in the car park?		How many gates are there?	
What is the number of *(red)* cars minus the number of *(silver)* cars?		How many steps are there around the school?	
What is the biggest number you can see take away 10?		How many rectangles are there on the *climbing frame?*	
What is the smallest number you can see add 10?		How many trees that are more than 2 metres high?	

Around the School Maths Trail – Year 3

Numeracy Focus: *Number. Geometry. Measurement. Problem solving*

Suitable for: Year 3 working in pairs

What you will need: Clipboards, trail sheets and pencils. Rulers.

What you do:

Use the template overleaf and add in the numbers and situations or locations relevant to your particular school where the text is in italics. You may like to put it in order of the way they will come across the answers.

Learning benefits:

- Children work independently in pairs
- Active learning
- Shows that Maths is everywhere
- Consolidates learning
- Supports NC 2014 Programmes of Study

Year 3 Maths Trail
Start at the main entrance gate

Names...

If you face the school entrance what do you see if you turn 2 right angles clockwise?		How many seats or benches are there?	
Estimate the height of the front entrance door.		If 30 children wanted to sit down how many benches would we need altogether?	
Add up the digits in the telephone number on the school sign.		Is the angle of the shelter roof acute or obtuse?	
What is the area of one of the paving slabs *on the path to the office?*		How many windows look out on the playground? What is half that number?	
How many cars in the car park have a number greater than 6?		What shape is the *??*	
What is 100 more than the number of cars in the car park?		How many gates are there? How many slats in all the gates?	
What is the number of *(red)* cars times the number of *(silver)* cars?		What fraction of the numbers on the number snake is odd?	
What is half the biggest number you can find?		What is the length of the swing seat?	
What is double the smallest number you can find?		How many bushes are < 1m in the border next to Class 1?	
How many symmetrical doors are there on the outside of the building?		Can you find a *(3D shape)?*	

Around the School Maths Trail Year 4

Numeracy Focus: *Number. Geometry. Measurement. Ratio. Problem solving*

Suitable for: Year 4 working in pairs

What you will need: Clipboards. Trail sheets. Pencils. Rulers.

What you do:

Use the template overleaf and add in the numbers, situations or locations relevant to your particular school, especially where the text is in italics. You may like to put the trail in order of the way they will come across the answers.

Learning benefits:

- Children work independently in pairs
- Active learning
- Shows that maths is everywhere
- Supports NC 2014 Programmes of Study for Maths

Year 4 Maths Trail
Start at the main entrance gate

Names...

If you face the school entrance what do you see if you turn 180° anti-clockwise?		How many seats or benches are there?	
What unit of measure would you use to measure the height of the arch of the porch?		If 50 children wanted to sit down how many more benches would we need?	
What is the tens digit x the hundred digit in the telephone number on the school sign?		Can you find a set of perpendicular lines on the playground? Where are they?	
What is the perimeter of two of the paving slabs **on the path to the office**?		How many windows look out on **the playground**? Divide that number by 2.	
How many cars in the car park have a number 6<8?		Can you find a (**3D shape**)? Where?	
What is 150 more than the number of cars in the car park?		How much taller than you is the top of the **climbing frame**?	
What fraction of the cars in the car park is **red**? What fraction is **silver**?		Draw the .... How many lines of symmetry does it have?	
Choose 4 digits from 2 number plates. What is the biggest number you can make with them?		Which angle is biggest – the apex (point) of the **shed roof** or a right angle?	
What is the smallest number you can see times 7?		Find an acute angle – where is it?	

Around the School Maths Trail Year 5

Numeracy Focus: *Number. Geometry. Measurement. Ratio.*
Problem solving

Suitable for: Year 5 working in pairs

What you will need: Clipboards. Trail sheets. Pencils. Rulers. Calculators

What you do:

Use the template overleaf and add in the numbers, situations or locations relevant to your particular school, especially where the text is in italics. You may like to put the trail in order of the way they will come across the answers.

Learning benefits:

- Children work independently in pairs
- Active learning
- Shows that maths is everywhere
- Supports NC 2014 Programmes of Study for Maths

Year 5 Maths Trail
Start at the main entrance gate

Names..

If you face the school entrance what do you see two right angles clockwise?		How many bricks are there in one metre square?	
Can you draw the shapes in the trellis **by the front door** accurately?		If we wanted to build a wall a metre long by 50cm high, how many bricks would we need?	
What is the biggest number you can make with the six digits in the telephone number on the school sign?		Estimate the angle of the ramp leading to **the girls' cloakroom** door.	
What is the area of one of the paving slabs **on the path to the office**?		How many rectangles make the windows which look out **on the playground** altogether?	
Which prime numbers can you find on the number plates in the car park?		What shape is the........	
What is the number of cars in the car park squared?		Estimate the perimeter of the school **fence.**	
Round the number of cars in the car park to the nearest 10. What is 2 tenths of that number?		Find 3 different types of triangle – where are they and what are they called?	
What is the biggest 2 digit number you can see on a car number plate?		How many doors are there on the outside of the building?	
What are its factors?		Face the door of **Class 4,** turn through 270°. What do you see?	

Around the School Maths Trail Year 6

Numeracy Focus: *Number. Geometry. Measurement. Ratio. Problem solving*

Suitable for: KS2 working in pairs

What you will need: Clipboards. Trail sheets. Pencils. Rulers. Calculators

What you do:

Use the template overleaf and add in the numbers, situations or locations relevant to your particular school, especially where the text is in italics. You may like to put the trail in order of the way they will come across the answers.

Learning benefits:

- Children work independently in pairs
- Active learning
- Shows that maths is everywhere
- Supports NC 2014 Programmes of Study for Maths

Year 6 Maths Trail
Start at the main entrance gate

Names..

If you face the school entrance what is 90° to your *left/ right?*		Stand on the playground and face the school, now turn 180°. What is facing you?	
Estimate how many metres it is from the school gate to the entrance?		If we wanted 60% of the school to be able to sit on a bench, how many more benches would we need?	
How many lines of symmetry do the school sign have?		Estimate how many roof tiles are there on the **staff room roof?**	
If four paving slabs cost £12 how much did the path **to the office** cost to build?		What proportion of the school windows look out on the playground?	
If 0.5 of the car park was iced over how many spaces would be available?		If each child needs 1sq metre to play on what is the maximum number who can play in the playground at any one time?	
If 1kg of road salt was enough to de-ice 2 car park spaces, how much would we need?		Collect two registration numbers that total 113	
What fraction of the cars is **(red)?**		If we wanted to put up 2 metre fence panels across the playground to divide it in half, how many would we need?	
What area of land does the **pond/ outside shed/**cover?			

Other resources from Thinking Child include:

Over 100 Ideas for Outdoor Literacy

Let's Think Homework

IT'S A CASE OF GRAMMAR

Starters for Thinking cards

The Literacy Box

The Numeracy Box

Visit the website: www.thinkingchild.org.uk

Or phone for more information: 01604 491511